# DATA COMMUNICATIONS & NETWORKING DICTIONARY

# DATA COMMUNICATIONS & NETWORKING DICTIONARY

• • • • • • • • • • • • • • • •

T.D. PARDOE

R.P. WENIG

Copyright © 1992 Professional Press Books

All rights reserved. No part of this publication may be reproduced, stored in a retrieval system, or transmitted in any form or by any means whatsoever, except in the case of brief quotations embodied in critical reviews and articles.

The information in this book is subject to change without notice and should not be construed as a commitment by the author or the publisher. Although every precaution has been taken in the preparation of this book, the publisher assumes no responsibility for errors or omissions.

Printed in the United States of America.

Cover design by Sue Ann Rainey

Library of Congress Cataloging-in-Publication Data

Pardoe, Terry D.
  Data communications & networking dictionary / T.D. Pardoe and R.P. Wenig.
    p. cm.
  ISBN 1-878956-06-X (softcover)
  1. Computer networks—Dictionaries.  2. Data transmission systems--Dictionaries.  I. Wenig, Raymond P.  II. Title.  III. Title: Data communications and networking dictionary.
  TK5105.5.P374  1992
  004.6´03—dc20                                         91-38380
                                                          CIP

Please address comments and questions to the publisher:

Professional Press Books
101 Witmer Road
Horsham, PA 19044
(215) 957-4287  FAX (215) 957-1050
Internet: books@propress.com

# Preface

During the last 15 years, our work in the communications industry has led us to confirm the popularly held view that every technology produces an abundance of its own abbreviations, acronyms, and elitist words. The unfortunate result is that simple concepts become difficult to understand, even by industry professionals. Nowhere, perhaps, is this problem more acute than in the rapidly expanding field of data communications and networking.

Further complicating the matter is that the electronic movement of data and the data's use within computer systems is based on many engineering disciplines, and the jargon in use is a combination of telephony, telegraphy, radio transmission, and computer hardware terminology. Sometimes the same word or abbreviation can mean two different things, and a single concept often is indicated by more than one word or acronym.

In this dictionary, we provide definitions of a wide range of communications and networking terms, from the very basic to the most complex. The dictionary is useful to the expert as well as the neophyte. Experts can quickly find the specific words, abbreviations, or acronyms they want. Neophytes will find all the help they need by turning to additional terms mentioned in the initial definitions. Abbreviations and acronyms are listed separately to assist in sorting out the "acronym soup," which at times can be both frustrating and misleading. Numerics are easily found in a separate section at the end of the dictionary.

Since networking standards are emerging at a rapid rate, we have included explanations of a wide range of the most often used standards, as well as information about the major sponsoring organizations. We recommend that you contact the appropriate standards organization directly if you need detailed information on a specific standard.

It is our hope that this dictionary will ease the process of sorting through and understanding specifications, proposals, and other material related to data communications and networking.

# A

**A and B signaling.** A technique used in T1 (1.544-Mbps) digital transmission systems to carry dial and control information within selected transmission frames. Bits are "robbed" from each of the subchannels to provide this facility.

**abbreviated address calling.** A calling method that allows the user to employ an address having fewer characters. The destination's assigned device addresses these characters when initiating a connection. May also be called abbreviated dialing when specifically used in connection with telephone systems.

**abbreviated dialing.** *See* abbreviated address calling.

**ABM.** *See* asynchronous balanced mode.

**ABX.** *See* advanced branch exchange.

**Academic Computing Research Facility Network (ACRFNET).** A network connecting various research units such as colleges and research and development laboratories in the U.S.

**access charge.** A Federal Communications Commission-specified charge for access to a local carrier either by a private-line user or a long-distance supplier.

**access code.** The digits that a telephone user must dial to obtain access to a specific service connection via a particular outgoing line. The eight or nine dialed on a hotel or company telephone is a good example.

**access control.** The process whereby a network or any of the components within it controls a using entity's (person, program, and so forth) access. The most common form of access control is the use of user identification numbers and passwords.

**access line.** The physical connection between an individual in-premises leased line and the local exchange or switching office of the provider of the leased line service. May also be referred to as the local loop.

**access network.** A subnetwork implemented to provide simple access to a more complex network. The access network often allows communication between a limited, local group of users and also additional access to a wider population.

**access routines.** Specific software routines that provide access to network resources.

**Accunet.** A 1.5-Mbps (T1) digital packet-switched network service offered by AT&T.

## Accunet Spectrum of Digital Services (ASDS)

**Accunet Spectrum of Digital Services (ASDS).** The name given by AT&T to its tariff schedules for Accunet services.

**ACD.** *See* automatic call distributor.

**ACF.** *See* advanced communications functions.

**ACK.** *See* acknowledge character.

**acknowledge character (ACK).** The encoded character used to acknowledge the error-free receipt of data. One of the many transmission control characters available in a code set.

**ACM.** Association for Computing Machinery.

**acoustic coupler.** A type of modem which generates audible tones so that computer-based data can be transferred onto a transmission medium using a standard telephone handset.

**acoustic delay line.** A line designed to delay audio signals by recirculating them in some type of medium. May also be called a sonic delay line.

**ACRFNET.** *See* Academic Computing Research Facility Network.

**ACSE.** *See* association control service element.

**ACU.** *See* automatic calling unit.

**A/D.** *See* analog-to-digital converter.

**adaptive routing.** A routing (switching) method that can adapt automatically to changes in the transmission facilities available within a network. This type of routing may, in a simple form, accommodate only failed lines or failed switching nodes. Varying traffic loads may be accommodated in a more complex form of this routing.

**ADCCP.** *See* Advanced Data Communications Control Protocol.

**ADCU.** *See* Association of Data Communications Users.

**address.** The unique identifier for a node (processor, switching point, and so forth) within a network.

**address family.** Any set of communications protocols that use the same addressing mechanism. May also be referred to as a protocol family.

**Address Resolution Protocol (ARP).** A Transmission Control Protocol/Internet Protocol process that maps Internet Protocol addresses to Ethernet physical addresses.

**adjacent devices.** Devices (or programs) within networks that are connected via a direct data link.

**adjacent domains.** IBM Corp. Systems Network Architecture domains that share a common Network Control Program.

**ADPCM.** *See* advanced differential pulse code modulation.

**advanced branch exchange (ABX).** A private branch exchange with advanced features normally including the ability to handle both voice and data in an integrated manner.

**advanced communications functions (ACF).** Software facilities which, when added to other system software, allow for the creation and operation of Systems Network Architecture networks between IBM Corp. computers.

**Advanced Data Communications Control Protocol (ADCCP).** A bit-oriented data link control protocol developed by the American National Standards Institute.

**advanced differential pulse code modulation (ADPCM).** A special form of pulse code modulation in which the modulation process is based on the previous signal, current signal and anticipated next signal.

**Advanced Peer-to-Peer Communication (APPC).** An IBM Corp. program which implements the Logical Unit 6.2 protocol set and controls transfers between like or unlike systems by treating them as equals. May also be referred to as Advanced Program-to-Program Communication.

**Advanced Peer-to-Peer Communication/PC (APPC/PC).** The software services required to implement APPC on PCs and the IBM Corp. Personal System/2.

**Advanced Peer-to-Peer Network (APPN).** A modification of IBM Corp.'s Systems Network Architecture specifications to accommodate the requirements of midrange computers, including the Application System/400.

**Advanced Research Projects Agency (ARPA).** The agency within the U.S. Department of Defense that supports the ARPANET network.

**AFIPS.** American Federation of Information Processings Societies.

**AFS.** *See* Andrew File System.

**aged packet.** A data packet which has exceeded its maximum predefined node visit count or time in the network.

**AIOD.** *See* automatic identification of outward dialing.

**airline miles (ALM).** The method used to calculate the distance (for rating purposes) of the point-to-point connections in the AT&T network.

**AIX.** The IBM Corp. version of the portable UNIX operating system.

**algorithm.** A mathematical model expressed as a set of rules or functional steps that is used to enable a computer to accomplish a specific task.

**allocation access.** A network access method whereby devices are allocated time on a transmission medium. The most popular LAN method is implemented by the use of a token and is used in the IEEE 802.4 and IEEE 802.5 LAN specifications.

**ALM.** *See* airline miles.

**Alohanet.** An experimental form of frequency modulation radio network developed by the University of Hawaii. Alohanet is implemented by creating transmission frames containing data, control information, and source and destination addresses which are broadcast for reception by a specifically defined destination.

**alternate buffer.** A temporary storage unit used to hold data when the primary buffer is full.

**alternate route.** A communications route used when the primary route is not available due to failure, congestion, and so forth.

**AM.** *See* amplitude modulation.

**American National Standards Institute (ANSI).** A standards-setting organization in the U.S. *Address*: American National Standards Institute, 1430 Broadway, New York, NY 10018.

**American Standard Code for Information Interchange (ASCII).** The way in which most non-IBM Corp. computers and digital devices encode real-world characters into a usable binary form. A number of different versions exist, including 7-bit ASCII (a maximum of 255 characters encoded) and 8-bit ASCII (7 data bits plus a parity bit).

**American Standards Association (ASA).** A U.S. standards-setting organization.

**American Telephone and Telegraph Company (AT&T).** A major supplier of telecommunications services and products in the U.S.

**American Wire Gauge (AWG).** A standardized method of specifying the size of wires. For example, home wiring is carried out using AWG #14 or #12, whereas telephone wire is normally AWG #22, #24, or #26.

**Ameritech.** One of the seven regional holding companies formed upon the divestiture of local telephone company service by AT&T. Ameritech is headquartered in Chicago and has an operational area covering the upper Midwest.

**amplifier.** A device that increases the strength of an analog signal without changing its form and information content.

**amplitude modulation.** The process whereby the amplitude (or strength) of an analog signal is varied to carry digital information. This modulation method is popular in low-cost modems.

**analog loopback.** A technique for testing transmission equipment and devices that isolates faults to the analog receiving or transmitting circuitry.

**analog signaling.** A type of signaling whereby information is represented in the form of an electrical, continuous picture of a physical event or series of events. For example, the output from a microphone is an electrical picture of the sound waves (pressure changes in the air) striking it.

**analog-to-digital (A/D) converter.** A device which converts continuous analog signals into discrete digital signals. In data communications, this device is normally referred to as a codec.

**Andrew File System (AFS).** A file access and transfer method created by Carnegie Mellon University and IBM Corp. that is being developed for use over the National Science Foundation 1.544-Mbps digital T1 network. AFS currently allows users at UNIX-based workstations to share files on a local network.

**ANI.** *See* automatic number identification.

**anisochronous transmission.** A transmission process in which there is always an integral unit of intervals between any two significant instants in the same group. A group may be a character or a block of characters.

**ANSI.** *See* American National Standards Institute.

**ANSI X3T9.5.** An ANSI standard defining aspects of a fiber-optic transmission system. Fiber-optic systems often are used as local area network backbones.

**answerback**. The process of transmitting a controlling character from a receiving device back to the transmitting device to signify readiness to accept data transmissions.

**antenna.** A device used to collect (receive) or radiate (transmit) high-frequency (radio) electromagnetic waves.

**APD.** *See* avalanche photodiode.

**API.** *See* application program interface.

**APPC.** *See* Advanced Peer-to-Peer Communication.

**APPC/PC.** *See* Advanced Peer-to-Peer Communication/PC.

**AppleTalk.** A network architecture developed by Apple Computer Inc. for use with the Macintosh computer. AppleTalk is primarily used in LAN applications to support additional file and print devices.

**application layer.** The layer of the Open Systems Interconnect (OSI) network architecture that performs the functions necessary to ensure the proper interaction between an application program and all other network and system software so that the desired end result is achieved. File access and transfer routines are examples of application layer functions.

**application program interface (API).** A set of software calls used by an application program to access network services.

**APPN.** *See* Advanced Peer-to-Peer Network.

**ARCNET.** A LAN method developed by Datapoint Corp. using 2.5-Mbps transmission and the token passing method of media access control.

**ARP.** *See* address resolution protocol.

**ARPA.** *See* Advanced Research Projects Agency.

**Arpac.** A CCITT X.25 packet-switched network operated in Argentina.

**ARPANET.** A wide area network using packet switching. The network was designed by ARPA within the U.S. Department of Defense to support the military and research communities. ARPANET currently is split into two loosely interconnected parts: Milnet, for military use, and the Internet, for commercial and academic use.

**ARQ.** *See* automatic request for retransmissions.

**ARS.** *See* automatic route selection.

# AT command set

**ASA.** *See* American Standards Association.

**ASCII.** *See* American Standard Code for Information Interchange.

**ASDS.** *See* Accunet Spectrum of Digital Services.

**ASR.** *See* automatic send/receive.

**association control service element (ACSE).** The International Standards Organization's Open Systems Interconnect (OSI) application layer services used, for example, in Manufacturing Automation Protocol V3.0.

**Association of Data Communications Users (ADCU).** A professional organization of data communications users headquartered in the U.S. The ADCU was formed to provide education to its members.

**asymmetrical modem.** A type of modem which uses the majority of the available bandwidth for data transmission and only a small portion for reception.

**asynchronous balanced mode (ABM).** A service of the data link level (Logical Link Control) in the IBM Corp. token-passing ring. ABM operates at the Systems Network Architecture data link control level and allows devices to send data link commands at any time.

**asynchronous gateway.** A device that allows for the attachment of a number of asynchronous terminal devices directly to a LAN.

**asynchronous time-division multiplexing (ATDM).** A time-division multiplexing method whereby devices use time on a transmission medium only when they have data to be transmitted. ATDM is more efficient than synchronous time-division multiplexing.

**asynchronous transmission.** The movement of binary bits across a transmission medium, where the transmitter and receiver have no common time reference. During asynchronous transmission it is normal to place controlling bits (framing) around each individual encoded character.

**asynchronous transmission mode (ATM).** The asynchronous transmission capability of a system capable of both synchronous and asynchronous transmission. For example, ATM is used to denote the asynchronous capabilities of Broadband Integrated Services Digital Network (B-ISDN) service.

**AT command set.** The *de facto* auto-dialing command set standard for most Bell 212A full-duplex, dial-up modems. The AT command set was developed by Hayes Microcomputer Products Inc.

# ATDM

**ATDM.** *See* asynchronous time-division multiplexing.

**ATM.** *See* automatic teller machine *and* asynchronous transmission mode.

**AT&T.** *See* American Telephone and Telegraph Company.

**AT&T Communications.** The AT&T division that operates the AT&T long-lines (inter-LATA) network.

**attenuation.** The loss of energy (strength) of a signal as it passes through a transmission medium. In the case of electrical transmission, the energy loss is the result of the electrical resistance offered by the specific medium. In electromagnetic and optical transmission, the loss is due to energy absorption by the medium.

**AT&T Technologies.** The AT&T division that manufactures communications equipment ranging from telephone handsets to private branch exchanges.

**audio frequency.** The range of frequencies detectable by the human ear.

**audiotex.** A process whereby a data-based computer delivers information to a voice mail system, which translates it into a spoken message.

**AUSTPAC.** A packet-switched network implemented in Australia.

**authentication.** The security processes which ensure that messages are complete, error free, and come from the claimed or stated source.

**auto-answer unit.** A device that normally attaches to a computer or other data source and is capable of answering dial network calls automatically.

**auto-dial unit.** A device that normally attaches to a computer or other data source and is capable of dialing a remote receiver automatically (on computer command).

**AUTODIN.** *See* Automatic Digital Network.

**automatic call distributor (ACD).** A voice telephone device that automatically distributes incoming calls to the correct destinations. Similar to, but simpler than, a private branch exchange.

**automatic calling unit (ACU).** A device capable of automatically initiating transmission "calls" (for example, a telephone auto-dial unit).

**Automatic Digital Network (AUTODIN).** A digital network operated by the U.S. Department of Defense.

**automatic equalization.** The process whereby the distortions produced by transmitting data in the form of a modulated analog signal are compensated for automatically.

**automatic fallback.** A modem's ability to negotiate an appropriate data rate with the modem on the other end of a link based on the transmission line quality.

**automatic identification of outward dialing (AIOD).** A private branch exchange service that identifies the calling extension to provide cost accounting data.

**automatic number identification (ANI).** The process of delivering the caller's number to the called party so that the caller can be identified.

**automatic request for retransmissions (ARQ).** A transmission control sequence that requests retransmission of data received in error.

**automatic restart.** 1. The mechanism whereby a process automatically restarts, after power failure, when power returns. Restart is from the exact point of interruption. 2. System facilities that allow restart from the point of departure after system failure.

**automatic route selection (ARS).** A private branch exchange service that allows for automatic selection of the most efficient and cost-effective route. May also be referred to as least-cost routing.

**automatic send/receive (ASR).** A teletypewriter that punches and reads paper tape offline and can transmit data from paper tape or a keyboard.

**automatic teller machine (ATM).** A device used in the banking industry to allow banking transactions to be carried out at a location remote from the bank's computer.

**Autonet.** A packet-switched network implemented in the U.S. by ADP. *Address*: ADP Autonet, 175 Jackson Plaza, Ann Arbor, MI 48106.

**availability.** A measure of how often a user finds a desired service available for use. Availability is most often expressed as a percentage of the maximum possible time.

**avalanche photodiode (APD).** A device used as a receiver in lightwave transmission systems.

**AWG.** *See* American Wire Gauge.

# B

**B8ZS.** A technique used to accommodate the ones density requirements of a public T1 transmission facility.

**babbling tributary.** A network station that continuously transmits meaningless information. In a more general sense, may be referred to as a babbling node.

**backbone.** 1. A term used in bus-based LAN technology to describe the major interconnecting bus. 2. Any network considered to provide interconnection among subnetworks.

**back-off.** The process whereby an attempt to perform a particular process is discontinued, most likely because a problem with the process was detected. In a communications sense, one example is the process whereby a transmitting station backs off (then tries again later) when a signal disruption of some form occurs.

**backup server.** A product, typically software, that ensures that at least the two most recent versions of a file are saved continuously.

**backward channel.** A transmission channel associated with, but used in the opposite direction to, a specific information transfer channel. A backward channel is used to carry supervisory or error-control data.

**balanced error.** The description of a facility which has a distribution of errors such that the mean value can be considered zero.

**balanced-to-ground line.** *See* balanced transmission line.

**balanced transmission line.** A line having conductors with equal resistance per unit length and equal capacitance and inductance between each conductor and ground. Coaxial cable is configured easily as a balanced transmission system by the use of resistance-to-ground terminators.

**balun.** Balanced/unbalanced. A device used in IBM Corp. wiring systems to interconnect balanced twisted-pair wires and unbalanced forms of coaxial cable.

**band.** The range of available frequencies defined by a higher and lower limit.

**bandpass filter.** A device that will only "pass" or conduct frequencies within a defined range referred to as the frequency band.

**band splitter.** A multiplexer designed to split the available frequency band into several independent channels suitable for data transmission.

**bandwidth.** The portion of a spectrum of frequencies which can be used effectively to transmit information. The term is sometimes used instead of effective bandwidth, which describes the maximum bit transfer rate through a specific medium.

**barrel connector.** A connector used to "straight line" connect two lengths of coaxial cable. In Ethernet installations where the number of connection nodes (for devices) is limited, a barrel connector normally counts as a node.

**baseband transmission.** 1. As used in LAN specifications, transmission at a single digital signaling rate. 2. In a general sense, any transmission whereby the information travels from source to destination in the same form in which it existed at the source.

**BASIC.** *See* Beginners All-Purpose Symbolic Instruction Code.

**Basic Input/Output System (BIOS).** Within the framework of the IBM Corp. personal computer and MS-DOS operating system, software/firmware services that provide the interface between applications and all serial and parallel input/output ports.

**basic mode link control.** The control of a data link using ASCII control characters as described by ISO IS 646 and CCITT V3.0.

**basic rate interface (BRI).** When used in conjunction with Integrated Services Digital Network technology, BRI is the interface used to connect telephone and terminal equipment to higher-order devices.

**basic service.** A U.S. Federal Communications Commission-defined set of minimal services provided by all local and long-distance telephone carriers. (The precise definition of what these services constitute is unclear.)

**batch processing.** A data processing method whereby all the data is collected and then offered to the computer for the most efficient processing.

**Batch Telecommunications Access Method (BTAM).** An access method used by non-Systems Network Architecture IBM Corp. systems.

**baudot.** An encoding method in which five bits are used to represent real-world characters.

**baud rate.** The signaling rate of a transmission medium. A 2,400-baud line carries 2,400 signal changes per second. This number may or may not be equal to the bit rate, depending on whether one signal change equals one bit. Baud is normally used in the singular form: 2,400 baud, not 2,400 bauds.

**BCC.** *See* block check character.

**BCD.** *See* binary coded decimal system.

**B channel.** Used with Integrated Services Digital Network (ISDN) technology, the B channel is a 64K-bps information-carrying channel.

**BDLC.** *See* Burroughs Data Link Control.

**beam splitter.** A device for splitting an optical transmission beam into two or more separate beams.

**beeper.** A device used to indicate to humans that they have a telephone or computer message waiting for them.

**Beginners All-Purpose Symbolic Instruction Code (BASIC).** A popular, end-user programming language heavily used with personal computers. BASIC was developed at Dartmouth College.

**bel.** A transmission control character used when there is a need to call for attention.

**Bell 103.** An AT&T modem specification for isochronous originate/answer transmission at 300 bps.

**Bell 113.** An AT&T modem specification similar to Bell 103 but offering originate or answer operation but not both.

**Bell 201.** An AT&T modem providing synchronous data transmission at 2,400 bps.

**Bell 202.** An AT&T modem specification providing asynchronous transmission at 1,800 bps.

**Bell 208.** An AT&T modem specification providing synchronous transmission at 4,800 bps.

**Bell 209.** An AT&T modem specification providing synchronous transmission at 9,600 bps.

**Bell 212.** An AT&T modem specification providing full-duplex asynchronous or synchronous data transmission at speeds up to 1,200 bps on the common carrier network.

**Bell 43401.** A Bell System publication that defines requirements for data transmission over limited distances on circuits supplied by the telephone company.

**Bell Atlantic.** One of the seven regional holding companies formed upon the divestiture by AT&T of its local telephone service supply companies. Bell Atlantic services the U.S. mid-Atlantic states.

# BIOS

**Bell Communications Research (Bellcore).** An organization formed upon divestiture by AT&T of it's regional telephone operating companies whose charter is to create telephone network standards and interfaces.

**Bell compatible.** A modem utilizing specifications created by the Bell Telephone System. These specifications are slowly being replaced by equivalent CCITT specifications.

**Bellcore.** *See* Bell Communications Research.

**Bell Operating Company (BOC).** One of the 22 telephone companies spun off from AT&T as a result of divestiture.

**BER.** *See* bit error rate.

**BERT.** *See* bit error rate test.

**beta test site.** The client site used to test products before they become available to the general population.

**BEX.** *See* broadband exchange.

**bias distortion.** A type of distortion in transmission systems that causes mark and space pulses to be lengthened or shortened.

**BI-bus.** The internal structure of the Digital Equipment Corp. VAX 8000 and VAX 6000 Series computers.

**binary code.** A pattern of logical zeros and ones used to represent real-world information.

**binary coded decimal system.** An encoding method in which the decimal digits are represented by four or six binary bits.

**binary phase shift keying.** A phase shift modulation technique.

**binary symmetric channel.** A channel designed so that the probability of changing binary bits in one direction is the same as the probability of changing them back to the correct state.

**Binary Synchronous Communications (BSC).** An IBM Corp. term for describing synchronized digital transmission.

**Binary Synchronous Communications Protocol (Bisync or BSCP).** An IBM Corp. data link control that utilizes various framing characters to implement control functions. It is a half-duplex protocol that exists in many versions, each of which is normally identified by a specific terminal type.

**BIOS.** *See* Basic Input/Output System.

**bipolar coding.** A transmission-level bit encoding method used by AT&T for T1 transmission at 1.544 Mbps or higher.

**bipolar waveform.** A transmission method that uses opposite polarity for successive mark (logical one) pulses and a neutral signal state for the space (logical zero) pulses.

**bis.** A qualifier added to the end of many CCITT recommendations showing that the indicated standard is an extension, normally with respect to performance, of another, similar standard. For example, CCITT V.22 is a standard that describes a modem operating at 600 and 1,200 bps. CCITT V.22bis designates a V.22 modem which has had its speed extended to 2,400 bps. *Note:* The bis designation is often incorrectly added in parentheses, as in CCITT V.22(bis).

**B-ISDN.** *See* Broadband ISDN.

**bit.** Binary digit. A specification of one of two possible states. The smallest possible unit of information.

**bit duration.** The time it takes one encoded bit to pass a specified point.

**bit error.** The term used to describe the condition where the value of a single bit is changed by conditions in the transmission medium.

**bit error rate (BER).** The ratio of bits received in error to the total number of bits transmitted.

**bit error rate test (BERT).** A control procedure designed to determine the number of bit errors encountered per unit time in a transmission system.

**BITNET.** A worldwide network connecting universities and other institutions of higher learning. The network connects more than 200 institutions and has more than 900 computational nodes.

**bit-oriented protocol.** A data link control protocol that uses specific bit patterns to transfer controlling information. Examples are IBM Corps.'s Synchronous Data Link Control (SDLC) and the CCITT High-Level Data Link Control (HDLC). Bit-oriented protocols are normally used for synchronous transmission only. Bit-oriented protocols are code transparent (meaning they work regardless of the character encoding method used), since no encoded characters are used in the control sequence.

**bits per second.** A measure of the transmission speed of a transfer system. The bit rate may not be the same as the baud rate, depending on how transmission-level encoding of logical ones and zeros is performed.

**bit stuffing.** A technique used to ensure that transmitted control information is not misinterpreted as data by the receiver during bit-oriented transmission. Additional binary zeros (or ones) are inserted at the transmitter after certain bit pattern transmission; such bits are then removed at the receiver. This technique may also be referred to as zero-bit insertion (or one-bit insertion).

**BLAST.** *See* Blocked Asynchronous Transmission.

**BLERT.** *See* block error rate test.

**block.** A set of characters normally stored or transmitted as a group.

**block cancel character.** A transmission control character used to indicate that all previous characters in the same block should be discarded.

**block check character (BCC).** The result of a transmission verification algorithm normally calculated during transmission and appended to the end of a block, then used for error detection by the receiver. Examples are cyclic redundancy check and longitudinal redundancy check.

**Blocked Asynchronous Transmission (BLAST).** A popular communications method that produces error-free transmission of blocks of data.

**blocked call.** A voice telephone control system or private branch exchange term indicating a call that cannot be completed because of a "network busy" condition.

**block error rate test (BLERT).** A control procedure designed to determine the number of erroneous blocks transmitted per unit of time.

**block-mode terminal interface (BMTI).** A device used to create (and break down) packets to be transmitted through a CCITT X.25 network. This device is needed if block-mode terminals (such as IBM Corp. Bisync devices) are to be connected to the network without an intermediate computer.

**block multiplexer channel.** An IBM Corp. mainframe input/output channel that allows interleaved blocks of data.

**BMTI.** *See* block-mode terminal interface.

**BNA.** *See* Burroughs Network Architecture.

**BNC connector.** A specific type of connector used for coaxial cable connection.

**BOC.** *See* Bell Operating Company.

**boot node.** A node within a network used to download operational software to other nodes so that they may operate.

**Border Gateway Protocol (BGP).** An Internet protocol defined by RFC 1163. BGP is a Transmission Control Protocol/Internet Protocol (TCP/IP) routing protocol for interdomain routing in large networks.

**boundary node.** In IBM Corp.'s Systems Network Architecture, a subarea node that can provide certain levels of protocol support for adjacent subarea nodes.

**bps.** *See* bits per second.

**BPSK.** *See* binary phase shift keying.

**break.** A long space, at least as long as a character, used for control purposes in certain asynchronous communications methods.

**BRI.** *See* basic rate interface.

**bridge.** 1. A device that connects network systems at the data link control level. Bridges are used extensively in LAN systems to extend their physical dimensions or modify their performance. 2. A general term used to describe devices that interconnect parts of the same logical network.

**bridge tap.** An undefined length of wire connected between the normal end points of a circuit, which introduces an unwanted modification of the transmission path characteristics.

**British Standards Institute (BSI).** A U.K. standards-setting organization concerned with a broad range of mechanical, physical, and operational functions.

**broadband exchange (BEX).** A service offered by Western Union providing data communications over channels of a customer-selected bandwidth.

**Broadband ISDN (B-ISDN).** An ISDN (Integrated Services Digital Network) service implemented on a broadband, analog transmission medium.

**broadband transmission.** 1. As used in LAN technology, the transmission of multiple analog signals at the same time over the same physical medium. 2. In a general sense, any transmission method in which data flows from source to destination in a different form than existed at the source.

**broadcast.** Transmissions radiated from a point throughout a carrying medium. Examples are radio wave broadcast from the transmitter in all directions, and wire-based broadcast from the transmitter in both directions to a terminator at each end of the conductor.

**broadcast medium.** A type of transmission medium that allows broadcast transmission to all points at the same time.

**broadcast message.** A message intended for all nodes within a network.

**brouter.** A local area network bridge with additional routing ability. A brouter may be able to provide least-cost routing or a minimal level of load balancing.

**BSC.** *See* Binary Synchronous Communications.

**BSCP.** *See* Binary Synchronous Communications Protocol.

**BSI.** *See* British Standards Institute.

**BTAM.** *See* Batch Telecommunications Access Method.

**buffer.** A temporary storage space used to hold data while decisions are made on its integrity and so forth.

**Burroughs Data Link Control (BDLC).** A bit-oriented data link control protocol similar to, but not the same as, IBM Corp.'s Synchronous Data Link Control.

**Burroughs Network Architecture (BNA).** A network architecture defined by Burroughs Corp., which along with Sperry Corp. is now part of Unisys Corp.

**burst mode.** A communications mode whereby a continuous stream (burst) of bits is transmitted without interruption.

**bus.** An electrical transmission circuit for carrying information or serving as a shared pathway or connection for a number of different devices.

**bus hog.** A slang term for a device connected to a transmission bus which, after gaining access to the transmission medium, transmits a large number of messages regardless of whether other devices are waiting.

**bus topology.** The network structure whereby connection between devices is accomplished by connecting all devices to a single transmission medium such as wire or fiber.

**busy hour.** The 60-minute period on a transmission link during any 24-hour day when the communications traffic is highest.

**bypass.** In common carrier voice network terms, the process whereby portions of the carrier's service are bypassed using customer-owned and operated facilities. Examples are microwave links between offices to interconnect telephone circuits before they are connected to telephone company transmission/reception points.

**bypass relay.** A relay used to bypass failed stations in a network. Bypass relay is of significant importance in a token-passing ring network.

**byte.** A set of eight bits. May also be referred to as an octet. A more general term than character, since computer and data communications devices often use eight-bit bytes, which do not have any real-world equivalent.

**byte count-oriented protocols.** Data link control protocols that use a data field byte count as part of their controlling information. A good example is Digital Equipment Corp.'s Digital Data Communications Message Protocol (DDCMP). This control method means that DDCMP can be used for either asynchronous or synchronous transmission.

**byte multiplexer channel.** An IBM Corp. input/output channel that interleaves data in bytes.

**byte multiplexing.** A form of time-division multiplexing in which a single byte from each attached device is sent down the transmission channel in successive time slots.

**byte stuffing.** The process whereby dummy bytes are inserted into a transmission stream so that the net data transmission rate will be lower than the actual channel data rate. The dummy bytes are identified by a single controlling bit within the byte.

# C

**cable.** A collection of metallic wires surrounded by an insulator through which an electric current can be passed.

**CAE.** *See* Common Application Environment.

**call-accepted signal.** A control signal transmitted by the called equipment to indicate that it accepts an incoming call.

**call-back modem.** A modem that the caller must activate with a password. It will then hang up and call back the caller's predefined number. Call-back modems are used to establish a level of security in dial-up systems.

**call detail recording (CDR).** A private branch exchange function that logs every call. Used for cost control reasons.

**call-division multiple access (CDMA).** A telephone equipment access control method.

**call forwarding.** A private branch exchange or common carrier service that allows for the automatic transfer of incoming calls (under a defined set of conditions) from one extension (device) to another.

**call-not-accepted signal.** A control signal transmitted by the called equipment to indicate that it cannot or will not accept an incoming call.

**call pickup.** A private branch exchange service that allows a user to answer a call from an extension other than the one which was called.

**call waiting.** A private branch exchange service that informs a station in use that it has another call waiting to be transferred.

**CAN.** *See* cancel.

**cancel (CAN).** A transmission control character used to indicate that the characters preceding it are in error and should be canceled.

**carriage return (CR).** The control character that returns the cursor on a CRT or the print head on a printer to the start position.

**carrier band.** The range of frequencies that can be modulated to carry information on a specific transmission system.

**carrier sense circuit.** A circuit used to detect the presence of a carrier signal on a transmission medium. It may or may not indicate whether data is being transmitted. Also referred to as carrier detect circuit.

## Carrier Sense Multiple Access with Collision Avoidance and Positive Acknowledgment (CSMA/CAPA)

**Carrier Sense Multiple Access with Collision Avoidance and Positive Acknowledgment (CSMA/CAPA).** A medium access control method used by some personal computer local area networks. The method uses a variety of techniques to reduce but not totally eliminate the possibility of message collisions. The use of positive acknowledgment eliminates any errors caused by collisions.

**Carrier Sense Multiple Access with Collision Detection (CSMA/CD).** An access method used in local area network technology that allows devices to contend for network access. A device that has data to transmit monitors the line (carrier sense) and transmits its data when it determines the medium is free (no transmissions from other stations). Since more than one device may attempt to transmit at the same time, this process can result in collisions. If a collision is detected during transmission, all the transmitting devices cease transmission and wait a period of time based on a control algorithm and then try again. This access method with a randomized exponential backoff is the medium access method specified in the IEEE 802.3 LAN specification.

**Carrier Sense Multiple Access with Collision Prevention (CSMA/CP).** A less popular form of medium access control than CSMA/CD, the access method used in the IEEE 802.3 specification.

**carrier signal.** A signal that carries no information in and of itself but that can be modified (by a modem, for example) to carry information.

**cascading faults.** Network faults that cause other network faults.

**CASE.** *See* computer-aided software engineering *and* common service application element.

**cathode ray tube (CRT).** A device used to display computer-generated or other information in a visual form.

**CATV.** *See* Community Antenna Television.

**C band.** The portion of the frequency spectrum —from 4 to 6 gigahertz— heavily used for satellite and microwave transmission.

**CBEMA.** Computer Business Equipment Manufacturers Association. *Address*: CBEMA, 311 First St. NW, Suite 500, Washington, DC 20001-2178.

**CBX.** *See* computerized branch exchange.

**CCIA.** *See* Computer and Communications Industry Association.

**CCIR.** *See* Comité Consultatif International de Radio (Consultative Committee for International Radio).

**CCIS.** *See* common channel interoffice signaling.

**CCITT.** *See* Comité Consultatif International Télégraphique et Téléphonique (Consultative Committee for International Telegraph and Telephone).

**CCITT V.3.** A specification that describes communications control procedures implemented in 7-bit ASCII code.

**CCITT V.21.** A specification that defines modems operating asynchronously at 200 or 300 bps in full-duplex mode on the dial-up network. Similar to the Bell 103 specification.

**CCITT V.22.** A specification that defines modems operating synchronously at 1,200 bps in full-duplex mode on the dial-up network. Similar to the Bell 212 specification.

**CCITT V.23.** A specification that defines modems operating asynchronously at 600 or 1,200 bps in half-duplex mode on the dial-up network and full-duplex mode on a leased circuit. Similar to the Bell 202 specification.

**CCITT V.24.** A physical layer interface specification that is the CCITT equivalent of EIA RS 232-C.

**CCITT V.26.** A specification that defines modems operating synchronously at 2,400 bps in full-duplex mode over leased lines. Similar to the Bell 201B specification. The recommendation specifies V.26ter, a special type of modem using public network-approved echo-back techniques.

**CCITT V.26bis.** A specification that defines modems operating synchronously at 2,400 or 1,200 bps in half-duplex mode over switched (dial-up) lines. Similar to the Bell 201C specification.

**CCITT V.27.** A specification that defines modems operating synchronously at 4,800 bps in half-duplex mode on the dial-up network and in full-duplex mode on leased lines. Similar to the Bell 208 specification. V.27bis specifies 2,400/4,800-bps modems. The V.27ter recommendation specifies modems using special echo-back techniques.

**CCITT V.29.** A specification for modems operating synchronously at 9,600 bps in full-duplex mode on a leased circuit.

**CCITT V.32.** A specification for modems operating at 9,600 bps on dial-up lines.

# CCITT V.33

**CCITT V.33.** A specification for modems operating at 14,400 bps on dial-up lines.

**CCITT V.35.** A specification that defines transmissions at 48 Kbps using 60- to 108-Kbps circuits.

**CCITT V.110.** A specification that defines the Integrated Services Digital Network (ISDN) support of data terminal equipment (DTE) that has a V-type interface.

**CCITT V.120.** A specification that defines a data link protocol for the B channel of an Integrated Services Digital Network (ISDN) network device interface.

**CCITT X.1.** A specification that defines classes of service in a packet-switched network, such as virtual-circuit, datagram, and fast-packet services.

**CCITT X.2.** A specification covering various aspects of user facilities in an X.25 packet-switched network.

**CCITT X.3.** A specification that defines the functions of the interface device needed for packet assembly/disassembly when using asynchronous terminals with CCITT X.25 packet-switched networks.

**CCITT X.20.** The physical layer specification for the connection of asynchronous devices to a CCITT X.25 packet-switched network. CCITT X.20bis is equivalent to EIA RS 232-C and allows connection to appropriate V series modems.

**CCITT X.21.** The physical layer specification for synchronous device connection to CCITT X.25 packet-switched networks. CCITT X.21bis is equivalent to EIA RS 232-C and allows connection to appropriate V series modems.

**CCITT X.24.** A list of definitions for interchange circuits between data terminal equipment (DTE) and data circuit terminating equipment (DCE) on public packet-switched networks.

**CCITT X.25.** The standard that defines the call-establishment and packet-transfer process for public packet-switched networks. The X.25 standard also references the full range of supporting services and their relevant standards, such as the standards related to addressing, data link control, and physical interfacing. The ISO equivalent is ISO 8208.

**CCITT X.28.** DTE/DCE interface for start/stop data terminal equipment accessing a packet assembly/disassembly facility on a public packet-switched data network in the same country.

**CCITT X.29.** A recommendation describing the rules for transfer between a packet assembly/disassembly device and standard data terminal equipment.

**CCITT X.32.** The interface between data terminal equipment and data circuit terminating equipment for packet-mode terminals accessing a public packet-switched data network via other telephone equipment.

**CCITT X.75.** A specification defining international interexchange signaling between packet-switched networks.

**CCITT X.92.** A specification defining a hypothetical reference interface for a packet-switched network.

**CCITT X.95.** A specification dealing with a number of internal packet-switched network parameters such as packet size limitations and service restrictions.

**CCITT X.121.** A specification that defines the international numbering scheme for network devices. X.121 is used by CCITT X.25 packet-switched networks and has been proposed by several computer vendors as the future universal addressing scheme.

**CCITT X.224.** A standard associated with the transport layer of the Open Systems Interconnect (OSI) architecture.

**CCITT X.225.** A standard associated with the session layer of the Open Systems Interconnect (OSI) architecture used in networks employing circuit-switched techniques.

**CCITT X.226.** A standard associated with the Open Systems Interconnect (OSI) architecture that defines specific presentation layer services used with circuit-switched network services.

**CCITT X.400.** A recommendation describing the form of an electronic mail message. The ISO equivalent is ISO 10021.

**CCITT X.401-430.** A series of recommendations for message-handling systems, including document content architecture and exchange formats. Similar services are defined by ISO 8613 and ECMA-101.

**CCITT X.500.** A recommendation describing X.400 message system directory support services. The ISO equivalent is ISO 9594.

**CCNET.** *See* Community College Network.

**CCR.** *See* Customer Controlled Reconfigurability.

**ccs.** Hundred (Roman numeral C) call seconds. A method of measuring traffic in a telephone system.

**CCSA.** *See* common control switching arrangement.

**CDMA.** *See* call-division multiple access.

**CDR.** *See* call detail recording.

**cell.** The area served by a single-frequency transmit/receive facility in a cellular radio system.

**cellular radio.** A method of producing limited area networks whereby radio frequency transmission is used to provide the communication channel from source to destination. The system is normally split into a number of cells operating at different frequencies. Each receive and transmit point is also connected by high-speed terrestrial lines (often 1.544-Mbps digital T1 circuits).

**centralized processing.** The method whereby data from various locations is moved to a single point for computer-based processing. The opposite of distributed processing.

**central office (CO).** A term used by common carriers when referring to switching points. May also be called local exchange or telephone exchange.

**central office local area network (CO-LAN).** Local area network service based on telephone company central office switching facilities.

**central processing unit (CPU).** A combination of the logic processor and timing control used as the basis of a digital computer. Commonly used to mean computer.

**Centrex LAN.** A common carrier-provided local area network service based on local exchange switching.

**Centrex service.** Central exchange service offered by a telephone company supplier. The switching between "in premises" communications is performed by a telephone company-owned remote switch.

**CEPT.** *See* Conference of European Postal and Telecommunications Administrations.

**channel.** A data communications path such as a wire, fiber-optic conductor, or broadcast frequency.

**channel attached.** The connection method whereby devices are connected directly to a computer's input/output channel.

# checksum

**channel bank.** When used in connection with T1 digital transmission technology, the device that connects equipment such as a private branch exchange to the T1 facility. In a general sense, a device that puts many low-speed signals onto one high-speed link and controls the transmission. Similar to the combination of a modem and a multiplexer on an analog line.

**channel capacity.** The maximum rate at which a channel can transmit data.

**channel service unit (CSU).** The device used by customer premises equipment to terminate a telephone company-supplied digital transmission line.

**character.** A group of bits used to represent a real-world character.

**character checking.** A method of checking for errors during transmission based on specific rules applied to individual characters.

**character code.** Any code set that represents a specific set of characters.

**character count.** An error control method whereby the number of characters in the data field of a transmission frame is recorded in the transmission frame header. May also be called byte count.

**characteristic impedance.** The termination impedance of a balanced transmission line that will minimize end-to-end reflections.

**character-oriented protocols.** Data link control protocols that use specific characters to carry control information. A good example is IBM Corp.'s Binary Synchronous Communications (BSC) protocol. Character-oriented protocols are used in both synchronous and asynchronous transmission.

**characters per second (cps).** A measurement of transmission speed in terms of characters transferred per unit time.

**character stuffing.** A technique used to ensure that transmitted control information is not misinterpreted as data by the receiver during character-based transmission. Special characters are inserted by the transmitter and then removed by the receiver.

**checksum.** A transmission control character used to detect errors. The checksum is a mathematical function of the data transmitted and is calculated at the transmitter, transmitted at the end of a stream of data, and then compared with a similar mathematically derived character produced by the receiver.

# CICS

**CICS.** *See* Customer Information Control System.

**CIM.** *See* computer-integrated manufacturing.

**circuit.** 1. A physical path along which electrons flow. 2. The physical-level connection between devices in the International Standards Organization (ISO) Open Systems Interconnect (OSI) model.

**Circuit Switched Digital Capability (CSDC).** A service implemented by the regional Bell Operating Companies that offers users a 56-Kbps digital service on a user-switchable basis.

**circuit switching.** The process whereby a circuit (actual or virtual) is switched into place at the inception of a telephone call or data transfer session and then maintained in place until the communication is discontinued. IBM Corp.'s Systems Network Architecture (SNA) uses circuit switching. The International Standards Organization (ISO) Open Systems Interconnect (OSI) reference model provides for both circuit switching and packet switching.

**Class n Office.** The way a telephone company defines its switching facilities. Class 5 is an end office (local exchange), Class 4 is a toll center, Class 3 is a primary switching center, Class 2 is a sectional switching center, and Class 1 is a regional switching center.

**class of service (COS).** A way of describing a network connection or communications link in terms of one of its many variables. Variables include such aspects as security, priority, and bandwidth.

**clear channel.** A transmission channel where the total bandwidth is available to the user. No part of the channel is needed for nonuser-generated control information.

**clear to send (CTS).** A physical-level control signal used by modems and other communications equipment signifying that transmission may begin.

**client.** 1. The user of a software service. 2. In the International Standards Organization (ISO) Open Systems Interconnect (OSI) specifications, the client is referred to as the service requester. 3. The hardware (workstation) or software that requests the computational services of a specific server.

**Cloax.** A high-performance, special-purpose coaxial cable designed by the Bell System.

**clock.** A transmission signal of precisely defined frequency or pulse rate used to synchronize a data transmitter and receiver. Also referred to as a clocking signal.

**closed user group.** A group of network users who can communicate only with other members of that group.

**cluster terminal controller.** A form of intelligent multiplexer that connects multiple terminals to a single high-speed line. The device also handles a number of data communications tasks and may implement data compression. In a Systems Network Architecture (SNA) environment, a cluster controller is a Physical Unit Type 2 device.

**CMA.** *See* Communications Managers Association.

**CMC.** *See* computer-mediated communications.

**CMIP.** *See* Common Management Information Protocol.

**CMOL/LLC.** *See* Common Management Information Protocol over Logical Link Control.

**CO.** *See* central office.

**coaxial cable.** A form of cable that has an inner conductor and an outer grounded shield positioned around a common axis. Coaxial cable has good noise immunity and is used for digital transmission up to 100 Mbps and for analog transmission up to 1,000 MHz.

**code.** A set of unambiguous rules specifying the manner in which data may be represented in a discrete form.

**codec.** A device used to convert analog (audio) signals to digital signals. In voice telephone systems, the most popular method is to take 8,000 samples per second and assign an 8-bit code to each. The result is 64-Kbps transmission.

**code conversion.** The process of changing the encoding for a specific character from one form to another.

**code-independent data communications.** A method of data communications that uses character-oriented data link control that does not depend on the character set or code used by the source.

**code-transparent data communications.** A method of data communications that uses a bit-oriented data link control protocol that does not depend on the bit sequence structure of the source.

**CO-LAN.** *See* central office local area network.

## collision

**collision.** In an IEEE 802.3 network, the presence of two transmissions on the channel at the same time is considered to be a collision.

**collision detect.** A method used in local area network technology to detect the presence of two or more signals on the channel at the same time. In baseband systems this process is simply a matter of determining the total energy level of the signal. One signal, one energy level; two signals, twice the energy level.

**Collision Free Packet Scheduling.** An AT&T local area network access method whereby frames are scheduled onto a bus-based network on the basis of predefined priorities. This process affords optimum utilization of the communications channel during periods of high load.

**colocation.** The process whereby equipment from multiple telephone company sources is located at the same place, usually to facilitate maintenance.

**COM1, COM2.** The communications input/output ports built into an IBM Corp. PC. The designation is used by MS-DOS, and internal interfacing is accomplished by the execution of Basic Input/Output System functions.

**combined station.** A term used in the High-Level Data Link Control (HDLC) protocol to describe a station that is either a primary or a secondary station.

**Comité Consultatif International de Radio.** Consultative Committee for International Radio. The CCIR is the group within the International Telecommunications Union concerned with standards and specifications in the broadcast medium communications industry.

**Comité Consultatif International Télégraphique et Téléphonique.** Consultative Committee for International Telegraph and Telephone. The CCITT is the group within the International Telecommunications Union concerned with the creation of standards and specifications in the contained medium (not the broadcast medium) communications industry. Address: General Secretariat, International Telecommunications Union, Place des Nations, CH-1211 Geneva 20, Switzerland.

**Common Application Environment (CAE).** The application environment created by the standard version of UNIX promoted by the X/Open group.

## Communications Managers Association (CMA)

**common carrier.** 1. A communications service supplier regulated in the public interest by the U.S. Federal Communications Commission. Examples include AT&T and MCI. 2. A communications service supplier rated and regulated in the public interest by a federal, state, or local utilities commission.

**Common Channel Interoffice Signaling (CCIS).** An AT&T method of controlling groups of trunks interconnecting central offices.

**common control switching arrangement (CCSA).** A private network service supplied by a common carrier that uses the same facilities as the public network.

**Common Management Information Protocol (CMIP).** A proposed set of network management services to operate in conjunction with the International Standards Organization (ISO) reference model for interconnected computers.

**Common Management Information Protocol over Logical Link Control (CMOL/LLC).** A proprietary network management method jointly developed by IBM Corp. and 3Com Corp. to manage devices on a mixed-media local area network.

**common service application element (CSAE).** A description used by the International Standards Organization (ISO) to describe certain application layer services. Examples are CCITT X.400 and ISO File Transfer and Access Method.

**Common Software Foundation (CSF).** A foundation developed by IBM Corp., Digital Equipment Corp., Hewlett-Packard Co., and other vendors to create a common system software interface upon which applications can be developed. The result should be improved interoperability among multivendor systems.

**communications adapter.** A device used to connect a computer to a communications facility directly or via another device such as a modem.

**communications control character.** A character used during data transmission to provide information about the data transmitted or to control the transmission process.

**communications controller.** An intelligent device used to offload the burden of communications from a computer. This device is normally located close to the computer it serves.

**Communications Managers Association (CMA).** A U.S. professional association serving the needs of communications managers.

**communications server.** An intelligent device providing communications services for a population of users. Heavily used in local area networks to provide access to wide area services.

**communications theory.** The mathematical discipline dealing with the probabilistic features of the transmission of messages in the presence of noise and other disturbances.

**Community Antenna Television (CATV).** A television distribution service utilizing broadband cable-based transmission. Otherwise known as cable TV.

**Community College Network (CCNET).** A special network implemented using Digital Equipment Corp.'s DECnet that interconnects community colleges in Pennsylvania, New York, and parts of Ohio.

**commutator. 1.** A device used in multiplexers (mechanical, electronic, or electro-mechanical) to connect the transmission line to various input channels. **2.** A device used in electric motors and generators to maintain current flow in one direction.

**ComNet.** A CCITT X.25 packet-switched network operated in the U.S.

**compander.** A contraction of the words "compressor" and "expander." A compressor is a device attached to telephone lines to compress the amplitude range of a signal at one point and expand it at another. A compander is used to improve signal-to-noise ratios.

**compatibility.** The state allowing for the accurate transfer of information from source to destination. (This does not imply that the destination will understand the information.)

**composite link.** A circuit carrying composite (multiplexed) data.

**compression.** The reduction of the number of bits required to define information during transmission.

**CompuServe.** A public access (subscription) database service that operates its own packet-switched network.

**computation server.** A network device used to provide computation (calculation) services for other network users.

**computer-aided software engineering (CASE).** The use of software to assist in the definition, design, and documentation of computer applications.

**Computer and Communications Industry Association (CCIA).** An industry association whose members are mostly equipment manufacturers.

**computer-based conferencing.** A conferencing method used between remote locations whereby all interaction is carried out using computer manipulation and displayed messages.

**computer-integrated manufacturing (CIM).** A systems approach to manufacturing whereby computers and communications networks are used to integrate individual operations.

**computerized branch exchange (CBX).** A private branch exchange that uses a small computer for control.

**computer-mediated communications (CMC).** The computerized process providing access and other support services in conjunction with computer conference systems or electronic mail networks.

**Computer Science Network (CSNET).** A network interconnecting more than 150 computer science and corporate research departments in the U.S.

**computer-to-PBX interface (CPI).** An interconnection device supplied by certain vendors to allow a computer to collect data from a private branch exchange.

**Comsat.** Communications Satellite Corp. A U.S. corporation established by statute as the exclusive U.S. communications satellite carrier.

**concatenation.** The process of linking several point-to-point circuits or channels to form a complete end-to-end connection.

**concentrator.** 1. An analog or digital device that reduces the number of trunks required. 2. A device that gathers messages from many lines and outputs them onto one line, usually at a higher speed. Its function is similar to that of a multiplexer.

**conditioned lines.** Telephone lines that have been modified by the carrier to improve their data-carrying capability. There are two types of conditioning: Type C conditioning corrects distortion and delays, and Type D corrects noise and harmonics.

**conditioning.** Modifications made to common carrier facilities to improve their data communications capabilities.

**Conference of European Postal and Telecommunications Administrations (CEPT).** A organization consisting of and representing the various European communications suppliers.

**congestion.** The condition in a packet-switched network when node transmission buffers are full and no more incoming packets can be accepted.

## congestion control

**congestion control.** The process whereby packets are discarded to clear buffer congestion in a packet-switched network.

**connection service.** A circuit-switching service whereby a connection is switched in place at the inception of a session and held in place until the session is completed. Also referred to as circuit switching. The circuit switched in place may be real or virtual.

**connectionless service.** Network service where no path can be identified between the transmitting source and the receiving destination at any point during a transfer. Datagram packet-switched networks provide connectionless service.

**connectivity.** The state that allows the transfer of electrical signals from source to destination.

**connector. 1.** An attachment at the end of a wire or set of wires that facilitates their connection to a device. **2.** In a general sense, any attachment that facilitates connection. **3.** In connection with token-ring local area network technology, a pattern of bits used to indicate the boundary between messages.

**connect time.** The amount of time a device is connected to a computer or network. Often used as a basis for determining service charges.

**contention. 1.** The result of multiple devices competing for limited services. **2.** A method used to implement medium access control in bus-based local area networks.

**contention access.** A network access method whereby devices contend for use of a transmission medium. A popular example is Carrier Sense Multiple Access with Collision Detection used in Ethernet and IEEE 802.3 LANs.

**continuously variable slope delta modulation (CVSD).** One of a number of techniques for encoding continuous analog voice signals into a digital form.

**control character.** A character transmitted for the purpose of transmission control.

**control station.** The station or node within a network that implements the various control functions that may be needed to ensure proper operation.

**conversational session.** A session wherein an operator sends a message and then awaits a reply before proceeding. Also called an interactive session.

**Corporation for Open Systems (COS).** The U.S.-based organization chartered to promote the use of International Standards Organization (ISO) and Integrated Services Digital Network (ISDN) standards within the U.S. *Address*: Corporation for Open Systems, McLean, VA 22102.

**COS.** *See* Corporation for Open Systems *and* class of service.

**COS Requirements Interest Group (COS RIG).** A group associated with a particular industry that helps the Corporation for Open Systems to effectively develop its conformance testing products and services.

**COS RIG.** *See* COS Requirements Interest Group.

**country code.** A set of digits in an address that signifies the destination country. Country codes may be internationally agreed upon, as with the telephone country code or the CCITT X.121 address used in X.25 networks, or may be vendor specific.

**CPE.** *See* customer premises equipment.

**CPI.** *See* computer-to-PBX interface.

**CPS.** *See* characters per second.

**CPU.** *See* central processing unit.

**CR.** *See* carriage return.

**CRC.** *See* cyclic redundancy check.

**crossbar switch.** An early form of matrix switching used by communications suppliers to implement circuit switching.

**crosstalk.** The undesirable transfer of a signal from one conductor to another.

**CRT.** *See* cathode ray tube.

**cryptography.** The process of transforming the representation of data to conceal its meaning. May also be referred to as encryption.

**CSAE.** *See* common service application element.

**CSDC.** *See* Circuit Switched Digital Capability.

**CSF.** *See* Common Software Foundation.

**CSMA/CAPA.** *See* Carrier Sense Multiple Access with Collision Avoidance and Positive Acknowledgment.

## CSMA/CD

**CSMA/CD.** *See* Carrier Sense Multiple Access with Collision Detection.

**CSMA/CP.** *See* Carrier Sense Multiple Access with Collision Prevention.

**CSNET.** *See* Computer Science Network.

**CSU.** *See* channel service unit.

**CTERM.** An application-level service in Digital Equipment Corp.'s DECnet protocol suite that implements the virtual terminal environment for network users.

**CTS.** *See* clear to send.

**current.** The amount of electrical charge (number of electrons) flowing past a specific point per unit time. The unit of measure is the ampere.

**current loop.** A method of transferring data between devices whereby a logical one is represented by a current of 20ma and the logical zero state is represented by no current.

**cursor.** A blinking symbol that indicates the current position on a CRT screen.

**Customer Controlled Reconfigurability (CCR).** An AT&T service that allows users to make changes in their network services.

**Customer Information Control System (CICS).** A transaction-based software system created and supplied by IBM Corp. and heavily used in commercial real-time applications.

**customer premises equipment (CPE).** The equipment installed at a customer site to interface with and connect to the common carrier's external facilities.

**CVSD.** *See* continuously variable slope delta modulation.

**cyclic redundancy check (CRC).** A complex number, which is a mathematical function of all the characters transmitted in a frame, that is transmitted at the end of the data stream and used by the receiver for error detection. The transmitted number is compared with an independently calculated but similar derived number at the receiver.

# D

**D4.** In T1 digital transmission technology, D4 is a fourth-generation channel bank. A channel bank is the interface between the T1 carrier system and a premises device such as a private branch exchange.

**D/A.** *See* digital-to-analog converter.

**DAA.** *See* data access arrangement.

**DACOMNET.** A packet-switched network implemented in South Korea.

**DACS.** *See* Direct Access and Cross Connect System.

**DAP.** *See* Data Access Protocol.

**DARPA.** *See* Defense Advanced Research Projects Agency.

**DAS.** *See* dual attachment station.

**DASD.** *See* direct access storage device.

**data.** 1. Any symbolic representation of facts (without interpretation). 2. Any representation such as characters or bits to which meaning may be assigned.

**data access arrangement (DAA).** Interfacing equipment supplied by a common carrier to allow privately owned communications equipment to be attached to that carrier's lines. The need for such equipment is eliminated if the customer devices are certified by the U.S. Federal Communications Commission.

**Data Access Protocol (DAP).** A high-level software service in Digital Equipment Corp.'s implementation of the Digital Network Architecture that provides for file access and transfer.

**data circuit transparency.** The capability of a circuit to transmit all data without changing its content or structure.

**DATACOM.** A data communications service offered by Western Union that provides relatively low-cost data transmission.

**data communications.** The movement of data by means of electrical (or photon, in the case of fiber optics) transmission systems.

**data communications equipment (DCE).** A term used extensively by the CCITT to describe a network interface.

**data compression.** The generic term for any one of a number of techniques used to reduce the number of bits transferred per unit time without modifying a message's informational content.

**data concentration**

**data concentration.** The process whereby data is collected, at a single point, from a number of low-speed communications lines for retransmission on a higher-speed line.

**DATACRC.** A cyclic redundancy check specifically associated with the data portion of a transmission frame.

**data directory.** A listing of the location of all stored information within a network. Location address information may be recorded as the physical location, the logical location (for example, a functional definition such as "financial data base"), or both.

**Data Distribution Management (DDM).** A set of rules defined by IBM Corp. for the exchange of data between dissimilar systems implemented using Advanced Peer-to-Peer Communication (APPC) software.

**data distribution system.** A system in which data stored in a central computer is sent to remote terminals continuously, in groups, or on demand.

**Data Encryption Standard (DES).** A U.S. federally approved method of encrypting data to provide limited levels of security.

**datagram packet network.** The type of packet-switched network in which each packet is individually routed. This may result in a loss of sequence within a message because of alternate distance routing, or a loss of portions of a message because of packet elimination for congestion control.

**data link.** Any serial, logical data communications transmission path between two devices.

**data link control (DLC).** The layer within the Open Systems Interconnect (OSI) architecture that performs the functions necessary to ensure reliable transmission across an unreliable physical link. Examples are Synchronous Data Link Control (SDLC) and High-Level Data Link Control (HDLC).

**data link escape (DLE).** A transmission control character used in IBM Corp.'s Binary Synchronous Communications (BSC) protocol. DLE is used in conjunction with a second character which denotes a specific control function.

**data link protocol.** The set of rules implemented at the data link control layer of a layered architecture and organized to create a "perfect" data transfer on an imperfect transmission medium. Major functions include startup, close down, flow control, and error detection and correction.

**data link protocol data unit (DPDU).** The form into which the data link control layer of an Open Systems Interconnect (OSI) network architecture will format data for use and recognition.

**data link relay.** Another name for a bridge. A device that transfers data link layer transmission frames from one network segment to another.

**DATANET 1.** A packet-switched network implemented in Holland and operated by the Dutch government.

**data network.** Any network of interconnected devices constructed and used for the transfer of data.

**data network identification code (DNIC).** A four-digit number that identifies specific services within a public data network.

**data over voice (DOV) transmission.** A method that allows data and voice to be transmitted at the same time on the same conductor. The data is transmitted by modulating a carrier whose frequency is well above the audio range. Voice signals are limited to 0 to 4 kilohertz by the transmitting equipment.

**data over voice frequency.** The frequency used to transmit data on the same transmission line as voice. Standards are not currently finalized, but a typical system uses 40 kilohertz (mark) and 36 kilohertz (space).

**DATAPAC.** A packet-switched network implemented in Canada. The network is owned and operated by Telecom Canada. *Address*: Telecom Canada, 410 Laurier Ave., Room 1160, Ottawa, Ontario KIP 6H5.

**DATAPAK. 1.** A packet-switched network implemented in Denmark and operated by the Danish government. **2.** A packet-switched network implemented in Sweden and operated by the Swedish government. **3.** A packet-switched network implemented in Finland and operated by the Finnish government. **4.** A packet-switched network implemented in Norway and operated by the Norwegian government.

**data PBX.** A private branch exchange designed specifically to switch data sources. May also be referred to as an active star controller.

**Dataphone-50.** A high-speed AT&T digital service that carries data at the rate of 50 Kbps.

**Dataphone Digital Service (DDS).** A digital transmission service supplied by AT&T.

**data rate.** A measure of transmission speed normally specified in bits per second.

## data service unit (DSU)

**data service unit (DSU).** A device used to connect computers directly to a common carrier-supplied digital service. May also be called a digital service unit.

**data set.** AT&T terminology for a modem.

**data set ready (DSR).** A physical-level control signal used by modems and other data communications equipment to signify to the attached equipment that a connection to the communications line has been made.

**data sharing.** The network service that allows users at different nodes to access data stored on one node in a network.

**data stream.** The flow of individual data bits being transmitted through a communications channel to accomplish the transfer of information.

**data switching exchange.** The equipment installed at a single location to provide circuit switching, packet switching, or both.

**data terminal equipment (DTE).** A term used extensively by the CCITT to describe devices that are connected to a network for the purpose of transmitting or receiving data.

**data terminal ready (DTR).** A physical-level control signal used by transmitting devices to notify modems that they are ready to transmit.

**data transfer rate.** The average flow of information per unit time from source to destination. The rate may be measured in terms of bits, bytes, blocks, frames, or packets per second, minute, or hour.

**data transmission interface.** A shared boundary defined by functional characteristics, common physical interconnection characteristics, signal characteristics, and other characteristics as appropriate.

**data transparency.** A facility provided by a data link control protocol that allows any pattern of bits, bytes, or characters to appear within the information field of a transmission frame and ensures that no pattern in this field will be treated mistakenly as control information by the receiver.

**data/voice multiplexer (DVM).** A device that combines voice and data signals on the same transmission line.

**DATEX P. 1.** An Austrian packet-switched network implemented and operated by the Austrian government. **2.** A packet-switched network implemented in West Germany and operated by the West German post office.

**dB.** *See* decibel.

**d-bit.** The delivery confirmation bit in an X.25 packet. It specifies whether or not confirmation of delivery is required.

**DC.** *See* device control characters *and* direct current.

**DCA.** *See* Defense Communications Agency, Distributed Communications Architecture *and* Document Content Architecture.

**DCE.** *See* data communications equipment.

**D channel.** In Integrated Services Digital Network (ISDN) technology, a channel outside of the normal information transfer bandwidth used for the transmission of control signals.

**DCM.** *See* digital circuit multiplexing *and* digital circuit multiplication.

**DCS.** A packet-switched network implemented in Belgium and operated by the Belgian government.

**DDCMP.** *See* Digital Data Communications Message Protocol.

**DDD.** *See* direct distance dialing.

**DDM.** *See* Data Distribution Management.

**DDN.** *See* Defense Data Network.

**DDS.** *See* Dataphone Digital Service.

**DDX-P.** A CCITT X.25 packet-switched network operated in Japan.

**decibel (dB).** A unit of measure of relative power used to describe levels of attenuation.

**DECnet.** The combination of hardware and software services used to implement Digital Equipment Corp.'s Digital Network Architecture (DNA).

**DECnet-DOS.** The software services that allow a computer running MS-DOS to participate in a DECnet environment.

**decoding.** The process whereby data which has been converted (encoded) in some form for transmission is returned to its original state.

**dedicated line.** A common carrier line reserved for the exclusive use of a predefined entity. Also used to describe any type of communications channel preassigned to a specific user.

**default parameters.** The set of parameters (for transmission control, for example) used if no parameters are set by the using entity.

## Defense Advanced Research Projects Agency (DARPA)

**Defense Advanced Research Projects Agency (DARPA).** The U.S. Department of Defense agency that oversees state-of-the-art projects.

**Defense Communications Agency (DCA).** An agency within the U.S. Department of Defense that assigns Internet addresses to hosts on the Defense Data Network.

**Defense Data Network (DDN).** A collection of networks that are administratively and physically distinct, including ARPANET and Milnet. Implemented and operated to support the strategic and administrative needs of the U.S. Department of Defense.

**delay.** The time between the initiation of an action and the observation of its effect. In data communications, for example, the time between the transmission of a signal at its source and its detection at the destination.

**delay distortion.** The distortion of an analog signal as it passes through a transmission medium. It is caused by different frequencies traveling through the medium at slightly different speeds.

**delay equalizer.** A device that adds a delay to analog signals, which will travel through a medium faster than other frequencies used to transmit portions of the same data. The objective is to create a medium that transfers all used frequencies in the same time over the same distance, thereby eliminating transmission delay distortion.

**DELNI.** *See* Digital Ethernet Local Network Interconnect.

**delta modulation.** A technique whereby a continuous signal is converted into a binary pulse pattern for transmission through low-quality channels.

**demarcation point.** The point defined under the terms of the AT&T divestiture agreement that marks the end of the customer premises and the beginning of the public network.

**demodulation.** The process of extracting information from a modified carrier signal.

**demodulator.** A device used to extract the useful information from a modulated carrier signal. The demodulation function is normally performed by the modulating device.

**DEMS.** *See* digital electronic message service.

**demultiplexer.** A device that separates the individual signals (from individual devices) that have been multiplexed onto a high-speed transmission system.

**departmental processing.** An approach to the supply of computer services to end users whereby computational power and information access is organized on a departmental basis. Such systems normally consist of combinations of computer types connected to a local area network.

**DES.** *See* Data Encryption Standard.

**destination.** The physical device that forms the end of a transmission path.

**destination address.** The address of the device to which data is sent by a transmitter.

**destination field.** The field in a transmission frame header that defines the destination address.

**destination service access point (DSAP).** The logical address of the specific service entity to which data must be delivered when it arrives at its destination. This information may be built into the data field of an IEEE 802.3 transmission frame.

**Deutsche Industrie Norm (DIN).** Translated, DIN means German Industrial Standard. DIN specifications are issued under the control of the German government. Some are used on a worldwide basis to specify, for example, the dimensions of a range of coaxial cable connectors.

**device control (DC) characters.** A set of control characters used for turning transmission/reception equipment on or off. Examples are DC1, DC2, and DC3. *See also* X-on/X-off.

**device driver.** The software or firmware that handles the data input to and output from a specific external device.

**D/I.** *See* drop and insert.

**DIA.** *See* Document Interchange Architecture.

**diagnostic.** A test by a program or other device used to test a device or service to validate that it is operating properly and to indicate error conditions.

**dial up.** The technique used to initiate a communications session over a common carrier switched transmission line.

**dial-up backup.** The use of two dial-up lines to replace a failed dedicated full-duplex circuit.

**dibit.** A group of two bits that can be used to represent four possible states. The states are represented as 00, 01, 10, and 00.

**DID.** *See* direct inward dialing.

**differential Manchester encoding.** A form of bit encoding used in some broadband LAN technology. *See also* Manchester encoding.

**differential pulse code modulation (DPCM).** A form of pulse code modulation whereby efficiency is enhanced by transmitting only the difference between the current signal strength and the previous pulse signal strength rather than the absolute values.

**differential transmission.** The process whereby information is carried as the difference in voltage between two transmission lines.

**Digital Circuit Multiplexing (DCM).** A technique developed by ECI Telecom Inc. to increase the capacity of transatlantic transmission cables.

**digital circuit multiplication (DCM).** A method of increasing the capacity of digital voice channels by utilizing the quiet time in a specific conversation to transfer other conversations.

**Digital Data Communications Message Protocol (DDCMP).** The data link control protocol used by Digital Equipment Corp. for point-to-point transmission. DDCMP may be used with asynchronous or synchronous transmission and uses a byte count method for error detection. It also uses pipelining and piggybacking to improve efficiency.

**digital electronic message service (DEMS).** An electronic mail message service based on cellular radio and cable TV facilities for metropolitan areas and satellite service for intermetropolitan area connection.

**Digital Ethernet Local Network Interconnect (DELNI).** The product offered by Digital Equipment Corp. that allows up to eight active devices to be connected to a single Ethernet transceiver. A similar device is manufactured by many other suppliers under various names. The DELNI can be thought of as "Ethernet in a box."

**digital loopback.** A technique used to isolate faults in the digital circuitry of a transmission system.

**digital microwave.** A microwave system in which most or all of the analog transmission facility is used for the transmission of digital signals.

**Digital Network Architecture (DNA).** The layered network architecture developed by Digital Equipment Corp. DNA is implemented with a combination of hardware and software products loosely referred to as DECnet.

## Digital Transport Protocol (DTP)

**Digital Signal Cross-connect Level 1 (DSX-1).** A telephone term used to describe the cross connection of DS-1 digital signal paths.

**digital signaling.** A form of signaling whereby information is represented in the form of discrete (on/off, high/low) signals.

**digital signal processor (DSP).** A microprocessor device used to process digital signals that were originally analog. For example, a digital signal processor may be used to compress a 64-Kbps voice signal (digitized with a codec) into a 4.8-Kbps signal.

**Digital Signal Service Level 0 (DS-0).** A telephone term for a 64-Kbps transmission facility or channel.

**Digital Signal Service Level 1 (DS-1).** A telephone term used in the U.S. for a 1.554-Mbps transmission facility or channel (synonymous with T1). In other parts of the world, DS-1 may refer to a 2.048-Mbps rate.

**Digital Signal Service Level 1C (DS-1C).** A telephone term used in the U.S. for a 3.152-Mbps transmission facility or channel.

**Digital Signal Service Level 2 (DS-2).** A general telephone term for a 3.152-Mbps transmission facility service or channel (synonymous with T2).

**Digital Signal Service Level 3 (DS-3).** A telephone term for a 44.736-Mbps transmission facility or channel (synonymous with T3).

**digital speech interpolation.** A voice compression technique that takes advantage of the natural pauses in human speech to multiplex more than one conversation onto the same transmission medium.

**digital switching.** The process whereby signals are routed through a network using switching devices constructed from digital logic circuits. The switching processes are then performed under stored logic (program) control.

**digital termination system (DTS).** A microwave transmission method used for short-distance digital transmission. Also called digital electronic message service.

**digital-to-analog (D/A) converter.** A device that converts digital signals into analog signals. In data communications systems, this process is performed by a modem.

**Digital Transport Protocol (DTP).** The network layer software module in Digital Equipment Corp.'s Digital Network Architecture (DNA).

## Digital Video Interface (DVI)

**Digital Video Interface (DVI).** A standard developed by Intel Corp. for the data compression of video images, whether transmitted or not.

**DIN.** *See* Deutsche Industrie Norm.

**DIP.** *See* dual in-line package.

**diplex.** A transmission method in which two signals are transmitted simultaneously in the same direction on a single conductor or channel. This is normally accomplished by using two different analog transmission frequencies.

**Direct Access and Cross Connect System (DACS).** Equipment manufactured by AT&T that allows for the interconnection of T1 transmission lines or of any of the separate 64-Kbps channels within separate T1 facilities.

**Direct Access Storage Device (DAS).** IBM Corp. terminology for storage devices externally attached to a computer.

**direct current (DC).** The flow of electrons at a constant level. A single, constant voltage applied across a conductor will produce a direct current.

**direct distance dialing (DDD).** The common carrier service that allows all subscribers to gain access to all other subscribers outside of their local area.

**direct inward dialing (DID).** A feature of some private branch exchanges that allows direct (from the outside) dialing to specific extensions without the help of an operator.

**direct outward dialing (DOD).** The ability of a private branch exchange to allow an extension to dial an outside number directly, without operator assistance.

**disk server.** A device that controls a disk and provides data storage and access services for a number of users. Disk servers are popular in local area network environments. Also called file servers.

**DISOSS.** *See* Distributed Office Support System.

**distortion.** The change in the shape of a signal as it passes through a transmission medium.

**Distributed Communications Architecture (DCA).** The network architecture defined by Sperry Univac and still supported by Unisys Corp. at some U.S. government installations.

## Document Interchange Architecture (DIA)

**distributed database.** A database that is physically distributed throughout a network to improve data access speed.

**Distributed Management Environment (DME).** A group of network management specifications endorsed by the Open Software Foundation (OSF).

**Distributed Office Support System (DISOSS).** A collection of IBM Corp. software products that support office automation functions.

**distributed PBX.** A private branch exchange system whose components are located throughout an organization and interconnected via a local area network.

**distributed processing.** The use of interconnected computers positioned such that the application-based work to be done is performed at the best physical and functional points throughout a network.

**distribution frame.** The wall-mounted frame used to terminate and cross connect telephone circuits.

**divestiture.** The breakup of AT&T mandated by the U.S. federal courts, effective January 1, 1984.

**DIX.** *See* DIX Ethernet.

**DIX Ethernet.** A standard version of the Ethernet LAN physical layer as agreed upon among Digital Equipment Corp., Xerox Corp. and Intel Corp. This specification is superseded (with various modifications) by the IEEE 802.3 specification.

**DLC.** *See* data link control.

**DLE.** *See* data link escape.

**DME.** *See* Distributed Management Environment.

**DNA.** *See* Digital Network Architecture.

**DNIC.** *See* data network identification code.

**Document Content Architecture (DCA).** A set of rules defined by IBM Corp. governing the formatting of the content of documents that are to be transferred in office automation systems.

**Document Interchange Architecture (DIA).** A set of rules defined by IBM Corp. governing the interchange of documents in office automation systems.

**DoD.** U.S. Department of Defense.

**DOD.** *See* direct outward dialing.

**domain.** 1. A collection of related nodes within a network. 2. As defined in IBM Corp.'s Systems Network Architecture (SNA), all the computational devices controlled by a System Services Control Point (SSCP).

**DOV.** *See* data over voice transmission.

**downline load.** Information transfer from one computer to another. *See also* download.

**downlink.** 1. The frequency channel used to transmit signals from a satellite to an earth station. 2. The transmission channel used to pass data from a large computer to a controlled subsystem.

**download.** The transfer of data, programs, or control characters from a large central computer to a small local computer using communications facilities.

**downtime.** Any period of time during which a service entity cannot provide its service.

**DPCM.** *See* differential pulse code modulation.

**DPDU.** *See* data link protocol data unit.

**DQBD.** A link-level protocol specified in the IEEE 802.6 metropolitan area network specifications.

**driver.** 1. A set of software routines used to control input and output ports. 2. Hardware circuits used to insert signals onto transmission lines.

**drop.** An available service point. Often used to describe the wiring in a network that is unique to a particular user.

**drop and insert (D/I).** In T1 digital transmission technology, the process whereby received signals are demultiplexed and then fed into a second multiplexer for further transmission.

**drop cable.** In local area networks, the cable used to connect a device interface to the backbone network.

**dropout.** A short period of time during which a transmission service looses the ability to transmit data. Bell System specifications define a dropout as any such loss which lasts for more than 4 milliseconds.

**dry T1.** A T1 circuit with an unpowered interface.

**DS-0.** *See* Digital Signal Service Level 0.

**DS-1.** *See* Digital Signal Service Level 1.

**DS-1C.** *See* Digital Signal Service Level 1C.

**DS-2.** *See* Digital Signal Service Level 2.

**DS-3.** *See* Digital Signal Service Level 3.

**DSAP.** *See* destination service access point.

**DSP.** *See* digital signal processor.

**DSR.** *See* data set ready.

**DSU.** *See* data service unit.

**DSX-1.** *See* Digital Signal Cross-connect Level 1.

**DTE.** *See* data terminal equipment.

**DTMF.** *See* dual-tone multifrequency.

**DTP.** *See* Digital Transport Protocol.

**DTR.** *See* data terminal ready.

**DTR/DSR flow control.** A flow control technique using the data terminal ready (DTR) and data set ready (DSR) control signals in the EIA RS 232-C interface.

**DTS.** *See* digital termination system.

**dual-attachment station (DAS).** A device used in token-ring networks to allow access to two separate cable systems at the same time, providing protection against cable failure or damage.

**dual in-line package (DIP).** The packaging method used for solid-state electronics whereby the connection conductors are placed on two parallel sides of the rectangular package.

**dual-tone multifrequency (DTMF).** The scheme used in touch-tone telephones whereby each depressed key generates two audio tones.

**duct system.** The mechanical enclosures used to hold and protect wires throughout a building.

**duty cycle.** The relationship between the time a device or facility is used and the time it is idle.

**DVI.** *See* Digital Video Interface.

**DVM.** *See* data/voice multiplexer.

**dynamic bandwidth allocation**

**dynamic bandwidth allocation.** A technique used to allocate transmission channels only to devices that are transmitting. It is used in some T1 multiplexer devices.

**dynamic routing.** A switching and routing technique that can be changed (or will change) as conditions in a network change.

# E

**EARN.** *See* European Academic Research Network.

**earth station.** The transmitting or receiving station used in satellite communications.

**EBCDIC.** *See* Extended Binary Coded Decimal Interchange Code.

**echo.** **1.** In terms of transmission control, an echo is the retransmission of received data. Echo-back techniques are used to ensure correct data entry. The echo may originate locally from a terminal or computer or remotely from a distant receiver. When an echo originates from a remote computer, the process may be referred to as echoplex. **2.** In a general sense, the component of any signal that, due to reflection or other reasons, arrives at the destination later than the main body of the signal.

**echo cancellation.** A process whereby some high-speed analog modems eliminate the effects of echo.

**echo check.** A method of checking the accuracy of data transmissions in which the received data is returned to the sending device for comparison with the original.

**echoplex.** The process whereby an echo of received characters is sent by the receiver back to the remote transmitting device.

**echo suppressor.** A device installed on a communications medium to reduce echoes to an insignificant level. Echo suppressors are particularly important in microwave transmission systems; they eliminate the effects of signals which are reflected from the receiving antenna back to the transmitter only to be rereflected back to the receiver.

**ECMA.** *See* European Computer Manufacturers Association.

**ECSA.** *See* Exchange Carriers Standards Association.

**EDI.** *See* electronic document interchange.

**effective bandwidth.** The maximum bit transmission rate through a specific medium.

**effective transmission rate.** The average number of bits, bytes, blocks and so forth per unit time transferred from the source to the destination and accepted as valid.

**EFT.** *See* electronic funds transfer.

**EHF.** *See* extremely high frequency.

**EIA.** *See* Electronic Industries Association.

**EIA RS 232-C.** An interface specification for the connection of computational equipment and data transmission equipment. EIA RS 232-C defines the electrical and physical characteristics and the set of signals needed to operate transmission lines, modems, and so forth and the conditions under which transmission can be started. In a layered network architecture, this interface is considered part of the physical layer.

**EIA RS 422-A.** A physical layer interface allowing for greater speeds and longer distances than those specified by EIA RS 232-C.

**EIA RS 423-A.** A physical layer interface specification that is compatible with EIA RS 232-C but that allows for faster speeds and longer transmission distances.

**EIA RS 442.** A variation of the EIA RS 449 physical layer interface.

**EIA RS 443.** A variation of the EIA RS 449 physical layer interface.

**EIA RS 449.** An electrical specification for a physical layer interface using unbalanced, voltage-defined digital signals.

**EIA/TIA 568.** An EIA standard for commercial building wiring. The standard covers four general areas: the medium, the topology of the medium, terminations and connections, and general administration.

**Eirpac.** A CCITT X.25 packet-switched network operating in Ireland under the control of the Irish government.

**EISA.** *See* Extended Industry Standard Architecture.

**electromagnetic interference (EMI).** Electromagnetic energy that leaks from or into any transmission medium. Coaxial shielding helps reduce both loss and pickup of such energy.

**electronic document interchange (EDI).** The process whereby standardized forms of documents are transferred between systems. The form and format of such documents may be defined by vendor specifications, CCITT standards, the ANSI X.12 standard, or the United Nations EDIFACT standard. EDI is also used in a general sense to refer to electronic data interchange.

**electronic funds transfer (EFT).** The process whereby banking data describing funds-based transactions is transferred between banking computer systems.

**Electronic Industries Association (EIA).** An organization concerned with standards in the electronics industry. *Address*: Electronic Industries Association, 1722 Eye St. N.W., Washington, DC 20006.

**electronic mail.** A message transfer system in which the information is transferred from source to destination in an electronic form. Electronic mail systems normally also provide a range of supporting services, including message storage and retrieval, message forwarding, and text editing.

**electronic software distribution (ESD).** The process whereby software distribution throughout a network is accomplished electronically using specially designed programs, called ESD programs.

**electronic switching system (ESS).** A switching system based on solid-state components and heavily used in AT&T and other telephone company networks.

**electronic tandem switch (ETS).** A telephone company switching device used to directly interconnect telephone company toll offices that are located in the same geographic area.

**EM.** *See* end of medium.

**EMA.** *See* Enterprise Management Architecture.

**EMI.** *See* electromagnetic interference.

**emulator.** A software or hardware product that imitates the performance of another device.

**encoding.** 1. The process whereby "real-world" characters are converted into bit code sets. 2. In voice transmission, the process whereby continuous analog signals are represented in a digital form. 3. In a general sense, the process whereby any entity is represented in terms of another entity.

**encryption.** The mathematical process whereby the data in a message is modified to protect it from illegal use.

**end node.** A network device that receives or transmits data but that does not perform routing functions.

**end of address (EOA).** A transmission control character used to signify the end of an address field.

**end of block (EOB).** A transmission control character used to signify the end of a block of data.

**end office.** another term for the local exchange operated by the telephone company.

**end of intermediate transmission block (ITB)**

**end of intermediate transmission block (ITB).** A transmission control character that signifies the end of an intermediate block used in IBM Corp.'s Binary Synchronous Communications (BSC) protocol.

**end of medium (EM).** A control character used to denote the end of the used (or useful) portion of a storage medium.

**end of message (EOM).** A framing character used in IBM Corp.'s Binary Synchronous Communications (BSC) protocol to signify the end of the current message.

**end of text (ETX).** A transmission control character that indicates the end of the current block of text as opposed to the total message.

**end of transmission (EOT).** A transmission control character signifying the end of a transmission.

**end of transmission block (ETB).** A transmission control character used to signify the end of a transmission block.

**end-to-end communications layer.** Another name for the transport layer in a layered network architecture. Used by Digital Equipment Corp. in the DECnet Phase IV implementation of the Digital Network Architecture (DNA).

**ENQ.** *See* enquiry character.

**enquiry character (ENQ).** A transmission character used to denote a request for a response from a remote station.

**Enterprise Management Architecture (EMA).** A network management architecture proposed by Digital Equipment Corp. and based on the International Standards Organization (ISO) Open Systems Interconnect (OSI) reference model. EMA allows for interconnection of all Digital products as well as many non-Digital systems.

**enterprise networking.** Information access in a multivendor network environment between a corporation's internal resources and its suppliers, customers, and other strategic partners.

**EOA.** *See* end of address.

**EOB.** *See* end of block.

**EOM.** *See* end of message.

**EOT.** *See* end of transmission.

**equal access.** The requirement, mandated by the U.S. Federal Communications Commission as a condition of the AT&T divestiture, that ensures that all U.S. long-distance suppliers have equal access to local loop exchanges.

**equalization.** A process used by most modems to improve the transmission characteristics of a communications medium.

**equivalent four-wire system.** A transmission system that uses separate frequency-derived channels to allow for full-duplex operation over one pair of wires.

**erlang.** The standard unit of telecommunications traffic capacity and usage demand. Named after A.K. Erlang, an employee of the British Post Office.

**error burst.** An unusually high rate of errors concentrated in a short period of time.

**error control.** The process by which a transmission system or network ensures reliable data transfer.

**error correction.** The mechanism used to correct detected errors in a transmission. Correction is normally achieved by retransmitting the information.

**error detection.** The process of detecting transmission errors by using simple parity checks or more complex cyclic redundancy checks.

**ESC.** *See* escape character.

**escape character (ESC).** A control character that alters the meaning of a limited number of continuously following bit combinations.

**ESD.** *See* electronic software distribution.

**ESF.** *See* Extended Superframe Format.

**ESS.** *See* electronic switching system.

**ET.** *See* exchange termination.

**ETB.** *See* end of transmission block.

**Ethernet.** The local area network technology developed by Xerox Corp. that uses the Carrier Sense Multiple Acess with Collision Detection (CSMA/CD) physical access method, special 50-ohm coaxial cable, and 10-Mbps digital transmission. *See also* DIX Ethernet.

## Ethernet controller

**Ethernet controller.** The unit that connects a device to the Ethernet cable. An Ethernet controller typically consists of part of the physical layer and much or all of the data link layer and the appropriate electronics.

**ETHERnim.** A Digital Equipment Corp. software product that provides management and performance-monitoring services in an extended local area network environment.

**ETS.** *See* electronic tandem switch.

**ETX.** *See* end of text.

**European Academic Research Network (EARN).** A European network connecting universities and other institutions of higher learning.

**European Computer Manufacturers Association (ECMA).** A European standards-setting organization. *Address:* ECMA, 114 Rue du Rhone, CH-1204, Geneva, Switzerland.

**even parity.** An error-checking process whereby all the transmitted characters are forced by the transmitter to have an even numeric value.

**exchange.** A telephone term used to describe the local telephone central office (switching point).

**Exchange Carriers Standards Association (ECSA).** A standards group under the American National Standards Institute (created before divestiture) consisting of regional operating companies and independent telephone companies.

**exchange termination (ET).** In Integrated Services Digital Network (ISDN) technology, ET refers to the central office link with the end user.

**exponential back-off delay.** The back-off algorithm used in IEEE 802.3 systems by which the delay before retransmission is increased as an exponential function of the number of attempts to transmit a specific frame.

**extended addressing.** One of many methods used to expand an address structure beyond its normal limit.

**Extended Binary Coded Decimal Interchange Code (EBCDIC).** An IBM Corp. method for encoding real-world characters into a usable binary form. The parity bit (for error detection) is imbedded in the code rather than added later as it is in ASCII code.

**Extended Industry Standard Architecture (EISA).** A 32-bit extension of the 8- and 16-bit internal bus structure developed by IBM Corp. The EISA bus was jointly developed by Compaq Computer Corp. and other personal computer (PC) manufacturers and is now the *de facto* standard for Intel Corp. 80286-, 80386-, and 80486-based PCs.

**extended LAN.** A local area network whose dimensions have been extended by the use of bridges.

**Extended Superframe Format (ESF).** A framing standard for T1 transmission proposed by AT&T. The extended format would improve error control and performance management.

**extension cable.** Any cable configuration used to extend the distance between connected devices.

**external modem.** A modem that acts as a standalone device as opposed to a modem installed within a computer.

**extremely high frequency (EHF).** Transmission frequencies in the range of 30,000 to 300,000 MHz.

# F

**facsimile (FAX).** Text or graphics transmitted via communications lines to a remote point where a hardcopy is reproduced. Transmission may be analog or digital.

**fading.** In microwave or radio transmissions, the process whereby the signal slowly diminishes due to electrical interference or atmospheric conditions.

**far-end crosstalk.** The transfer of signals between conductors that then travel in the same direction as the signals, causing problems at the far end.

**fast-packet multiplexing (FPM).** A form of time-division multiplexing that deals with packetized data from multiple channels and multiple source types. Unlike standard time-division multiplexing, a fast-packet device can favor channels (for example, a voice channel) based on source type and interrupting channels (for example, a data channel) to allow higher-priority signals, such as voice, to be transmitted first.

**fast-packet switching.** A packet-switching service that can transfer both voice and data.

**fast select.** A service available on CCITT X.25 networks whereby a short message can be included in the set-up messages and delivered even if the requested transfer session is not completed.

**FAX.** *See* facsimile.

**FCC.** *See* Federal Communications Commission.

**FCS.** *See* frame check sequence.

**FDDI.** *See* Fiber Distributed Data Interface.

**FDM.** *See* frequency-division multiplexing.

**FDX.** *See* full-duplex transmission *and* frequency-division multiplexing.

**FE.** *See* form effectors.

**FEC.** *See* forward error correction.

**Federal Communications Commission (FCC).** A board of five individuals appointed by the president of the United States and charged with the task of regulating communications within the U.S.

**Federal Communications Standard (FED-STD).** A designator used to describe standards developed by the FTSC.

# fiber loss

**Federal Information Processing Standards (FIPS).** The identifier attached to standards developed to support the U.S. government computer standardization program. The FIPS effort is carried out by the U.S. Department of Commerce. *Address:* U.S. Department of Commerce, National Technical Information Service, 5285 Port Royal Rd., Springfield, VA 22161.

**Federal Telecommunications Standards Committee (FTSC).** A U.S. government agency established in 1973 to promote standardization of communications and network interfaces. FTSC standards are identified by the designator FED-STD. *Address:* General Services Administration, Specification Service Administration, Bldg 197, Washington Navy Yard, Washington, DC 20407.

**FED-STD.** *See* Federal Communications Standard.

**FED-STD-1001.** A Federal Telecommunications Standards Committee (FTSC) standard for high-speed synchronous signaling.

**FED-STD-1002.** An FTSC standard for time and frequency references in networks.

**FED-STD-1003-A.** An FTSC standard for a bit-oriented synchronous data link control protocol. Also called Advanced Data Communications Control Protocol (ADCCP).

**FED-STD-1005.** An FTSC standard for the coding and modulation requirements of a specific 2.4-Kbps modem.

**FED-STD-1006.** An FTSC standard for modulation requirements of a specific 4.8-Kbps modem.

**FED-STD-1007.** An FTSC standard for the coding and modulation requirements for a specific 9.6-Kbps modem.

**FED-STD-1008.** An FTSC standard for the coding and modulation requirements for duplex 600-bps and 1.2-Kbps modems.

**FEP.** *See* front-end processor.

**FF.** *See* form feed.

**Fiber Distributed Data Interface (FDDI).** An interface to a fiber-optic distribution medium that conforms to the IEEE 802.8 specifications. The implementation of this interface should make possible the creation of a supernetwork connecting many local area networks.

**fiber loss.** The energy loss in a light signal caused by its transmission through a fiber-optic medium.

**fiber-optic medium.** A transmission medium constructed using fine glass fibers, through which information (data) is transferred using light waves created by a laser or light-emitting diode.

**file separator (FS).** A control character used to designate the end of a file.

**file server.** A network device that services the filing needs of other network nodes. File servers may also be referred to as disk servers. (File serving is one of many services that can be provided using a disk server.)

**File Transfer and Access Method (FTAM).** Rules by which data can be accessed in remote files and part or all of the files can be transferred between systems. FTAM may also be called File Transfer Method (FTM).

**File Transfer Method (FTM).** A set of rules by which files are transferred from one system to another under the control of a UNIX system.

**File Transfer Protocol (FTP).** An upper-level service used in the Transmission Control Protocol (TCP) environment that allows for and manages the process of file transfer across a network.

**filter.** An electronic device that removes a specific frequency or group of frequencies from a transmitted signal. Filters are typically used to eliminate predefined types of noise.

**FIPS.** *See* Federal Information Processing Standards.

**FIPS PUB.** *See* FIPS Publication.

**FIPS PUB 1-1.** The FIPS standard for an information interchange code based on the American Standard Code for Information Interchange (ASCII).

**FIPS PUB 7.** The FIPS standard for the implementation of the FIPS information interchange code.

**FIPS PUB 15.** The FIPS standard for subsets of the FIPS information interchange code.

**FIPS PUB 16-1.** The FIPS standard for bit sequencing for the FIPS information interchange code.

**FIPS PUB 17-1.** The FIPS standard for the character structure and parity sense of the FIPS information interchange code.

**FIPS PUB 22-1.** The FIPS standard for synchronous signaling rates between transmitting and receiving devices.

**FIPS PUB 37.** The FIPS standard for high-speed synchronous signaling rates between transmitting and receiving devices.

**FIPS PUB 46.** The FIPS standard for data encryption.

**FIPS PUB 71.** The FIPS standard for a data link control procedure. The same as ADCCP (Advanced Data Communications Control Protocol).

**FIPS PUB 78.** The FIPS standard for the implementation of ADCCP.

**FIPS Publication (FIPS PUB).** The designator used for documents that describe standards developed by the Federal Information Processing Standards group within the U.S. Department of Commerce.

**firmware.** A series of program steps required to implement a specific function that are stored in read-only memory.

**flag.** A bit or set of bits used in transmission framing to alert intermediate or final systems that special conditions apply to the transmission or that specific actions must be taken.

**flooding.** A packet-switched network routing method whereby identical packets are sent to all destinations to ensure that the intended destination is reached.

**floppy disk.** A flexible plastic disk coated with magnetic material that can be used to store information.

**flow control.** The process by which the flow of messages or data is controlled within a system. Packet flow control in a packet-switched network, for example, is the responsibility of the transport layer, whereas data frame flow control in a point-to-point connection is the responsibility of the data link layer.

**FM.** *See* frequency modulation.

**FM subcarrier.** One-way data transmission using the modulation of an unwanted portion of an FM broadcast station's frequency band.

**Foreign Exchange Service (FX).** A common carrier service providing subscriber connection to an exchange other than the normal local exchange.

**format.** The specific way in which data is ordered so that a receiver can understand its position-related content.

**form effectors (FEs).** A group of control characters intended for the control of the layout and format of data on an output device such as a printer or CRT. Examples are CR (carriage return) and LF (line feed).

**form feed (FF).** A control character used to advance a printing device by one total form or page.

**forward bandpass.** The range of frequencies in a broadband transmission system used to transmit outgoing signals from an attached device.

**forward channel.** The transmission channel that carries data or voice from the caller to the called entity.

**forward error correction (FEC).** The process whereby additional bits are appended to each character as it is transmitted so that the receiver will be able to detect and correct transmission errors. The most commonly used FEC process results in the ability (at the receiver) to detect and correct 100 percent of all single bit errors and to detect but not necessarily correct approximately 99.99 percent of all multiple bit errors.

**four-wire circuit.** A transmission system consisting of four wires, two for each transmission direction.

**FPM.** *See* fast-packet multiplexing.

**fractional T1.** A T1 service whereby the customer leases a 128-, 256-, 384-, or 512-Kbps channel that is part of a T1 transmission system owned by the telephone company.

**fractional T3.** A telephone company service in which portions of a T3 (44.7364-Mbps) transmission service are leased to provide a service similar to a T1 (1.544-Mbps) or T2 (3.152-Mbps) channel, but normally at a lower cost.

**frame.** The entity transferred from transmission source to destination across a physical link and defined by the data link layer protocol.

**frame check sequence (FCS).** A multibit (16- or 32-bit) error-checking code appended to the end of a transmission frame in bit-oriented data link protocols.

**frame relay.** A service proposed by long-haul carriers that will transfer data link layer transmission frames from a defined source to a defined destination. Frame-relay service is important as a means of improving performance in extended local area networks.

**framing.** The process of placing control information around characters or messages before transmission. For asynchronous transmission, individual characters are framed. For synchronous transmission, blocks of data or messages are framed.

**freeze frame.** The process whereby a limited number of digital image frames are captured and transmitted per second. The freeze-frame technique is used in teleconferencing to reduce transmission bandwidth requirements.

**frequency.** The rate, in hertz, at which a signal pattern is repeated.

**frequency agile modem.** A modem that has the ability to search a broadband transmission system and find an available frequency-derived channel. The modem then modulates analog signals at that frequency.

**frequency band.** A specified range of available frequencies.

**frequency-division multiplexing (FDM).** A method whereby several low-speed devices are able to share a single transmission line by using different analog transmission frequencies.

**frequency hopping.** The process whereby several communications channels of different frequencies are used for the same data transmission.

**frequency modulation (FM).** The process of varying the frequency of an analog signal to carry digital information. FM is the most popular modulation method for modems designed for use with analog telephone lines.

**frequency offset.** Nonlinear distortion that causes a shift in the frequency of a received signal.

**frequency response.** The frequency range that can be properly transmitted without excessive distortion.

**frequency shift keying (FSK).** An alternate term for frequency modulation.

**front-end processor (FEP).** A processing device between a computer and a network of terminals or other computers. Its main function is to implement the controls needed for communication. An FEP may also provide some level of computational backup. When its sole function is communications control, the FEP may be called a communications controller.

**FS.** *See* file separator.

**FSK.** *See* frequency shift keying.

**FTAM.** *See* File Transfer and Access Method.

**FTM.** *See* File Transfer Method.

**FTP.** *See* File Transfer Protocol.

**FTSC**

**FTSC.** *See* Federal Telecommunications Standards Committee.

**full-duplex transmission (FDX).** Transmission in both directions at the same time (bidirectional).

**fully connected network.** A network in which each node is connected directly to every other node. The number of connections required to create a fully connected network is $(n)(n-1)$ divided by 2, where $n$ is the number of nodes in the network.

**FX.** *See* Foreign Exchange Service.

# G

**gain.** A measure of amplification, normally expressed as the ratio between output energy and input energy.

**gain hit.** The condition whereby a telephone line exhibits a sudden increase in power such that data transmission capability is lost. The Bell System has established the maximum duration and frequency of such occurrences allowed within a defined period of time.

**garbled transmission.** Transmission that has so many errors that no information can be gathered from it.

**gateway.** The hardware or software product that allows access from one networked system environment to another. (This term is often used to describe a device that interconnects networks at any level.)

**Gaussian noise.** Undesirable and random electromagnetic noise introduced into a medium that may disrupt transmission.

**gender.** Connectors are assigned a gender to describe their physical type. Connectors with pins are considered male, and those with sockets are considered female.

**gender changer.** A special connector used to modify the gender of the plug (socket) required to connect to a specific socket (plug).

**geosynchronous orbit.** A satellite orbit whose position above the earth is such that the satellite rotation speed and the earth's rotation speed are the same. The result is that the satellite appears to be stationary above a fixed point on the earth's surface.

**GOSIP.** *See* Government OSI Profile.

**Government OSI Profile (GOSIP).** A U.S. government interagency network architecture that specifies UNIX-derived upper-level services and the International Standards Organization (ISO) Transport Protocol Class 4 (TP4) as the transport layer. Development of the U.S. GOSIP standards is under the control of the National Bureau of Standards (NBS).

**graphical user interface (GUI).** A communications link or interface between a user and a computer's operating system. GUIs use pull-down menus and icons (representative pictures) to help the user accomplish specific tasks.

**gray code.** A code used for translating certain analog representations into binary representations, such as the representation of angle. Gray code may also be called cyclic binary code or reflective code.

**ground.** A circuit connection to the earth.

**ground station.** The earth-based transmission or reception point in a satellite communications system.

**Group III FAX.** A facsimile standard specifying a transmission speed of 9,600 bps. At this speed, 20 seconds are required to transmit an 8.5-inch by 11-inch page.

**Group IV FAX.** A facsimile standard specifying a transmission speed of 64 Kbps. At this speed, six seconds are required to transmit an 8.5-inch by 11-inch page.

**group addressing.** The use of addresses that are common to two or more receiving stations.

**guard band.** The narrow frequency band left vacant between adjacent channels to prevent cross-channel interference and improve channel identification.

**GUI.** *See* graphical user interface.

# H

**half duplex (HDX).** The type of transmission whereby a device can receive or transmit but not at the same time.

**hamming code.** A code that uses redundant bits as a means of detecting transmission errors.

**handle.** A popular term used in place of the word "name." In the Transmission Control Protocol/Internet Protocol (TCP/IP) environment, handle is used to describe the temporary identification given to an entity so that it can be called and used.

**handshaking.** The two-way transfer of predefined control information required to start a communications session.

**hardware.** A set of electronic components interconnected so that the whole will perform a specifically defined task or set of tasks.

**hard-wired.** Describes a connection between two or more devices that is direct and permanent.

**harmonic distortion.** The distortion of a signal as it passes through a transmission medium. It is caused by the creation of additional harmonic frequencies.

**HASP.** *See* Houston Automatic Spooling Program.

**HDLC.** *See* High-Level Data Link Control.

**HDRCRC.** A cyclic redundancy check associated with a transmission frame header.

**HDX.** *See* half duplex.

**head-end converter.** A device used in broadband transmission systems that receives signals at one frequency, performs amplification, and then transmits the signal at a different frequency.

**header.** The control information in a transmission frame that precedes the data field. Sometimes abbreviated to HDR.

**heartbeat.** In an IEEE 802.3 network, a circuit (normally part of the transceiver) that generates a collision signal at the end of a transmission. This signal is used by the controller interface for self-testing purposes.

**hertz.** A measure of frequency. The same as cycles per second.

**heuristic routing.** A routing method that examines the delays suffered by incoming packages in a packet-switched network and forwards the packets along routes that will optimize their end-to-end transmission time.

**hexadecimal numbering system**

**hexadecimal numbering system.** A numbering system with the base 16, whose digit set, which includes six letters, is 0 1 2 3 4 5 6 7 8 9 A B C D E F. (Compare this with the base 10 numbering system, whose digit set is 0 1 2 3 4 5 6 7 8 9.) The base 16 numbering set is used to represent the combinations of four binary bits to simplify the overall representation of computer instructions or data.

**HF.** *See* high frequency.

**high-capacity service.** Generally used to describe public, tariffed, digital transmission service at speeds greater than T1.

**high frequency (HF).** Describes transmission frequencies in the range of 3 to 30 megahertz.

**High-Level Data Link Control (HDLC).** A data link control protocol defined by the International Standards Organization (ISO). HDLC is similar to IBM Corp.'s Synchronous Data Link Control (SDLC).

**high pass.** A frequency level above which an analog filter allows all frequencies to pass.

**holding time.** The length of time a specific communications channel is in use to accomplish a particular transfer.

**Hollerith Code.** A method of encoding real-world information so that it can be represented by punched holes on an 80-column card. This code is named after its inventor, Herman Hollerith (1860-1929).

**homogeneous network.** A network consisting of a series of a single type of device.

**hop.** A general term used to describe a single point-to-point connection within a network.

**host node.** The computer within a network that provides a range of services to other devices within the network.

**hot potato routing.** A packet-switching routing technique that retransmits a package as soon as possible after reception, even if it means making a poor routing choice, such as a choice based on time or cost.

**Houston Automatic Spooling Program (HASP).** A control protocol used by IBM Corp. to transfer files and jobs from peripheral devices to IBM 360 and IBM 370 processors.

**hub.** A device from which a number of transmissions links radiate. A hub-based network has the same configuration as a star topology.

**HUI.** *See* human interface.

**human interface (HUI).** 1. in a general sense, any device or facility that allows humans to interact with network devices or services. 2. As used in the definition of the proposed multivendor integration architecture sponsored by Nippon Telephone and Telegraph (NTT) Co. of Japan, HUI relates to any set of standardized services that allow humans to interact with a complex integrated system.

**hunt group.** A group of telephone lines, each with separate numbers but accessible via a single telephone number, allowing one directory listing to cover all lines. All lines would have to be busy before a potential caller would receive a busy signal.

**hybrid network.** 1. A network that combines analog and digital signaling. 2. A network that combines local and global connections. 3. A network comprising more than one architecture. 4. Any combination of the networks just described.

# I

**IAB.** *See* Internet Activities Board.

**IAB-IETF.** *See* IAB Internet Engineering Task Force.

**IAB Internet Engineering Task Force (IAB-IETF).** The engineering subsidiary task force within the Internet Activities Board.

**IAB Internet Research Task Force (IAB-IRTF).** The research subsidiary task force within the Internet Activities Board.

**IAB-IRTF.** *See* IAB Internet Research Task Force.

**IBERPAK.** A CCITT X.25 packet-switched network operated in Spain by the Spanish government.

**IBM 3270.** An IBM Corp. terminal. This is a popular device to emulate to create a connection between non-IBM systems and IBM computers.

**IBM Interconnect.** A set of software services that allow a non-IBM Corp. computer to operate in an IBM environment.

**IBM S/370 Channel Connection.** A direct connection via the bus system to an IBM Corp. computer with a System/370 architecture.

**ICA.** *See* International Communication Association *and* International Communications Association.

**ICMP.** *See* Internet Control Message Protocol.

**IDCMA.** *See* Independent Data Communications Manufacturers Association.

**IEC.** *See* interexchange carrier.

**IEEE.** *See* Institute of Electrical and Electronics Engineers.

**IEEE 801.1.** The IEEE local area network specification that describes the terminology to be used when defining networks.

**IEEE 802.2.** The IEEE local area network specification for the logical link control, which defines a specific format for data and interfaces to one of a series of IEEE-specified physical layers.

**IEEE 802.3.** The specification for the physical layer in a local area network that uses the Carrier Sense Multiple Access with Collision Detection (CSMA/CD) access method, has a bus configuration, and uses baseband transmission. IEEE 802.3 is based on original DIX Ethernet specifications.

**IEEE 802.4.** The specification for the physical layer in a local area network that uses the token-passing access method, has a bus configuration, and uses broadband transmission. IEEE 802.4 is specified as one of the transmission methods that may be used in the Manufacturing Automation Protocol (MAP) architecture.

**IEEE 802.5.** The specification for the physical layer in a local area network that uses the token-passing access method, has a ring configuration, and normally uses baseband transmission. IEEE 802.5 is used in IBM Corp.'s implementation of token-ring technology.

**IEEE 802.6.** The specification for a metropolitan area network.

**IEEE 802.8.** The specification for a Fiber Distributed Data Interface (FDDI) to be used to connect devices to a fiber transmission system using the token-passing access method.

**IEEE 802.11.** A proposed standard for line-of-sight, wireless-based local area networks.

**IFIPS.** *See* International Federation of Information Processing Societies.

**IMP.** *See* interface message processor.

**Impac.** A CCITT X.25 packet-switched network operated in the U.S.

**impedance.** The combined effect of the electrical resistance, capacitance, and inductance of a transmission medium.

**impedance discontinuity.** A point at which the electrical properties of a transmission medium change. Impedance discontinuity is important because at high frequencies it may result in reflections and malfunction.

**impulse hit.** A voltage spike in a telephone transmission line that causes a transmission error. Certain Bell System standards define the allowable number and size of such hits in a predefined period of time.

**independent data communications.** Any data communications control method that operates independently of the character encoding used by either the transmitter or receiver.

**Independent Data Communications Manufacturers Association (IDCMA).** A U.S membership organization dedicated to promoting and protecting the needs of independent communications equipment manufacturers (those not aligned with AT&T).

**INFONET.** A packet-switched network implemented in the U.S. *Address:* INFONET, 2100 Grand Ave., El Segundo, CA 90254.

**information interchange.** Any process whereby information is exchanged between entities without alteration of content.

## Information Systems Network (ISN)

**Information Systems Network (ISN).** An AT&T local area network technology that uses a collision-free contention scheme for medium access control.

**Infoswitch.** A CCITT X.25 packet-switched network operated in Canada.

**infrared.** The portion of the electromagnetic spectrum just beyond the visible red. Infrared is used for fiber-optic transmission and some short-haul "free air" communications.

**inside wiring.** A term often used in place of customer premises wiring.

**Institute of Electrical and Electronics Engineers (IEEE).** A U.S. professional organization active in the creation, promotion, and support of communications specifications and standards. *Address*: IEEE Computer Society, 5855 Naples Plaza, Suite 301, Long Beach, CA 90803.

**integrated information system.** A network of interconnected computers and databases in which any computational device can access any and all data stored within the network, subject to security and privacy restrictions.

**Integrated Services Digital Network (ISDN).** A type of network that transfers all information from source to destination in a digital form. The network is generally formed using a combination of circuit- and packet-switched facilities. When offered by a common carrier, the network-to-user interface is defined by the CCITT 1.100 series of recommendations.

**integrated voice and data terminal (IVDT).** A terminal device with a data interface, keyboard, and display, as well as a voice interface and telephone handset, which normally is attached to a single communications channel. Communication is voice over data or vice versa, and the terminal normally works in conjunction with a specific private branch exchange.

**INTELPAK.** A packet-switched network implemented in Hong Kong and operated by the Hong Kong Telephone Company.

**Intelsat.** The International Telecommunications Satellite Consortium, an organization of member nations formed in 1964 and dedicated to the creation and maintenance of a worldwide communications satellite network.

**interactive system.** A computer-based system that processes transactions as they occur.

## International Federation of Information Processing Societies (IFIPS)

**interactive terminal interface (ITI).** A device used to create packets to be transmitted through a CCITT X.25 network and to break down packets received from a CCITT X.25 network. This device is needed if nonintelligent asynchronous terminals are to be connected to the network without the use of an intermediate computer.

**interconnect company.** A company that supplies equipment to connect user-owned devices to a common carrier network.

**interexchange carrier (IEC or IXC).** Any common carrier licensed by either the U.S. Federal Communications Commission or a state utility commission to carry transmission between local telephone areas. Examples are AT&T Long Lines, MCI, and U.S. Sprint.

**interface.** The point at which two dissimilar entities are brought together. Interfaces may be created between dissimilar hardware devices or software functions.

**interface message processor (IMP).** An interfacing device used to connect various computers to the ARPANET network. The IMP provides the end-to-end control needed to ensure the integrity of transferred data in a multivendor environment.

**interface unit identification.** A security procedure whereby a transmitted message carries a definition of the transmitting device.

**interference.** Noise or other distortion during the transmission of data which may cause errors.

**intermediate system.** Another name for a router.

**Intermediate System-to-Intermediate System Protocol (IS-IS).** A protocol set proposed by the International Standards Organization (ISO) for use in controlling transfers between routers on dissimilar networks.

**intermodulation distortion.** A transmission effect that causes a signal to appear at the extremes of its voltage swing at the zero level.

**International Communication Association (ICA).** An international organization of academic institutions concerned with the promotion and use of international communications facilities.

**International Communications Association (ICA).** An international organization of communications equipment manufacturers.

**International Federation of Information Processing Societies (IFIPS).** An international organization concerned with the promotion of processing standards.

## International Record Carrier (IRC)

**International Record Carrier (IRC).** One of a group of carriers that, until recently, was part of a monopoly of U.S. common carriers certified to carry data and text to locations outside the U.S. In recent years, regulation of this type of service has been relaxed.

**International Standards Organization (ISO).** An international standards-setting organization. *Address*: ISO, Central Secretariat, 1 Rue de Varembe, Case Postale 56, CH-11211, Geneva 20, Switzerland.

**International Telecommunications Union (ITU).** An international, treaty-based organization concerned with telephone and telegraphic standards. The original organization, The Union Télégraphique, was formed in 1865; the current name was adopted in 1947. Standardization of procedures, processes, and equipment is handled by one of two groups within the organization: The Consultative Committee for International Telegraph and Telephone (CCITT) handles contained medium-based systems, including data communications, and the Consultative Committee for International Radio (CCIR) handles broadcast communications systems.

**International Telecommunications Users Group (Intug).** An international users group dedicated to the promotion and use of telecommunications and the satisfaction of users' needs.

**Internet Activities Board (IAB).** An independent committee of researchers and professionals with a technical interest in the proper evolution of the Internet system. Internet refers to the network layer services used in the Transmission Control Protocol/Internet Protocol (TCP/IP) environment.

**Internet Control Message Protocol (ICMP).** The Transmission Control Protocol/Internet Protocol (TCP/IP) process that provides the functions needed for network layer management and control.

**Internet Protocol (IP).** A network layer protocol developed in conjunction with the Transmission Control Protocol (operating at the transport layer), originally in the ARPANET network, which is now supported by many versions of UNIX and used by a wide range of network operating systems.

**internetwork.** A single, logical network formed by connecting two or more dissimilar networks.

**internetwork device.** Another name for a gateway.

**Internetwork Packet Exchange (IPX).** A network layer protocol developed by Novell Inc. and used in NetWare implementations.

**interoffice trunk.** A direct connection between telephone company central offices.

**interoperability.** The process whereby computers can operate interactively with each other across a network without data conversion or human intervention.

**interpacket gap.** The time interval between successive data packets in a transmission system.

**interrupt.** A signal used to interrupt an ongoing process so that another process, defined in some way by the interrupt, can be executed. After the second process is complete, the interrupted device returns to the original process.

**interstate communication.** Communications between U.S. states. Communication across state lines is regulated by the Federal Communications Commission.

**Intug.** *See* International Telecommunications Users Group.

**I/O.** input/output.

**IP/TCP.** An alternate name for TCP/IP (Transmission Control Protocol/Internet Protocol). IP/TCP may be used when referring to the software that implements the set of TCP/IP protocols.

**IPX.** *See* Internetwork Packet Exchange.

**IRC.** *See* International Record Carrier.

**IS.** A category of transmission control characters used to separate and qualify data logically. The meaning attributed to each character must be assigned by presentation or session layer services at the time of use.

**isarithmic control.** A flow control method used in packet-switched networks whereby the number of packets moving within the network at any point in time is held constant. This is one of the many methods used to implement congestion control.

**ISDN.** *See* Integrated Services Digital Network.

**IS-IS.** *See* Intermediate System-to-Intermediate System Protocol.

**ISN.** *See* Information Systems Network.

**ISO.** *See* International Standards Organization.

**ISO 646.** The ISO specification for the 7-bit character encoding set for information processing interchange.

# ISO 2022

**ISO 2022.** Code extension methods for ISO 7-bit code.

**ISO 2110.** The ISO standard for 25-pin transmission interface designation and pin assignments. The CCITT equivalents are V.24 and V.28.

**ISO 2593.** The ISO standard for connector pin allocations for use with specific high-speed data transmission equipment. The CCITT equivalent is V.35.

**ISO 3309.** The ISO specification for the frame structure for High-Level Data Link Control (HDLC) procedures. The ECMA equivalent is ECMA-40.

**ISO 4903.** The ISO standard for a 15-pin transmission interface and pin assignments. The CCITT equivalents are the X-series interfaces.

**ISO 8073.** The ISO specifications for transport layer services in networks conforming to the Open Systems Interconnect (OSI) architecture. Several classes of service are available. The most popular is Class 4 service, often abbreviated to TP4. The CCITT equivalent is X.224. The ECMA equivalent is ECMA-72.

**ISO 8208.** An ISO standard defining the lower three layers of the Open Systems Interconnect (OSI) architecture when used with public packet-switched network connections. The CCITT equivalent is X.25.

**ISO 8326/8327.** ISO specifications for session layer service and protocols in circuit-switched networks conforming to the Open Systems Interconnect (OSI) architecture. The CCITT equivalent is X.225. The ECMA equivalent is ECMA-75.

**ISO 8348.** An ISO network layer standard covering the circuit-switching process.

**ISO 8348 AD1.** An ISO network layer standard covering certain packet-switching processes.

**ISO 8348 AD2.** An ISO network layer standard covering specific address format issues.

**ISO 8472/3.** The ISO specification for the network layer of a packet-switched network conforming to the Open Systems Interconnect (OSI) architecture. The ECMA equivalent is ECMA-92.

**ISO 8571.** The ISO specification for file access and transfer, an upper-layer function for networks conforming to the Open Systems Interconnect (OSI) architecture.

**ISO 8602/8072.** The ISO specification for a transport layer service in networks conforming to the Open Systems Interconnect (OSI) architecture, which uses connectionless service (packet-switched service) at the lower layers.

**ISO 8613.** An ISO application layer standard for document content architecture and interchange format for letters, memos, and business reports transferred through office automation systems. The CCITT equivalents are the CCITT T.410 series and CCITT T.73. The ECMA equivalent is ECMA-101.

**ISO 8649/8650.** An ISO application layer standard covering protocol issues involved with the provision of a range of common application support services.

**ISO 8802.2.** The ISO equivalent of IEEE 802.2.

**ISO 8802.3.** The ISO equivalent of IEEE 802.3.

**ISO 8802.4.** The ISO equivalent of IEEE 802.4.

**ISO 8802.5.** The ISO equivalent of IEEE 802.5.

**ISO 8823.** An ISO presentation layer standard associated with circuit-switched network services. The CCITT equivalent is X.226.

**ISO 8881.** An ISO network layer standard covering protocols associated with various aspects of X.25 services in local area network environments.

**ISO 9040/9041.** An ISO application layer standard covering the protocols associated with virtual terminal services.

**ISO 9314-1.** An ISO physical layer standard covering transmission protocols in a medium-independent FDDI (Fiber Distributed Data Interface) transmission system.

**ISO 9314-2.** An ISO data link layer standard covering medium access control protocols in an FDDI (Fiber Distributed Data Interface) transmission system.

**ISO 9314-3.** An ISO physical layer standard covering transmission protocols in a medium-dependent FDDI (Fiber Distributed Data Interface) transmission system.

**ISO 9579.** An ISO application layer standard specifying the services needed to perform remote database access.

## ISO 9594

**ISO 9594.** An ISO application layer standard for the directory services associated with an electronic mail system. The CCITT equivalent is X.500.

**ISO 9596.** An ISO application layer standard covering the network management communication between management processes and management agents in lower Open Systems Interconnect (OSI) layers.

**ISO 10021.** An ISO application layer standard for the message-handling services needed in an electronic mail system. The CCITT equivalent is X.400.

**ISO 10589.** An ISO network layer standard covering the protocols associated with the intermediate-to-intermediate system transfer process at the network layer.

**isochronous transmission.** Any transmission method in which there is a fixed and constant time interval between any two significant events.

**ITAPAC.** A CCITT X.25 packet-switched network operated in Italy.

**ITB.** *See* end of intermediate transmission block.

**ITI.** *See* interactive terminal interface.

**ITU.** *See* International Telecommunications Union.

**IVDT.** *See* integrated voice and data terminal.

**IXC.** *See* interexchange carrier.

## J

**jacket material.** When used in connection with a transmission cable, the material used as the outer insulator.

**jam.** In an IEEE 802.3 network, the jam signal, which is normally produced by fixing the minimum number of data bytes that must be transmitted, is used to ensure that if a collision is produced, all devices on the network will detect it.

**J-bit.** An encoded transmission bit, produced by differential Manchester encoding, that does not represent data and is used only for transmission control.

**J-carrier system.** A transmission system carrying 12 telephone channels that uses frequencies up to 140 kilohertz.

**jitter.** Temporary effects caused by instability in a transmission system.

**Joint Photographic Expert Group (JPEG).** When the JPEG acronym is used in conjunction with video data, it refers to a technique for data compression that may be used regardless of whether the data is transmitted.

**JPEG.** *See* Joint Photographic Expert Group.

# K

**K.** When used as a computer measurement, such as K bytes of memory, K represents the numeric value 1,024.

**ka band.** The portion of the electromagnetic spectrum in the 18 to 30 gigahertz per second range.

**k-bit.** An encoded transmission bit produced by differential Manchester encoding, which represents data and is used only for transmission control.

**k-carrier system.** A transmission system providing 12 voice telephone circuits on a bandwidth of up to 60 kilohertz.

**Kermit.** A set of data link and higher-level software protocols developed to facilitate file transfer. The software, written at Columbia University, is in the public domain and therefore is inexpensive.

**kernel.** When referring to system software, the kernel is the software that interfaces directly with the hardware. For example, the Open Systems Interconnect (OSI) session layer kernel interfaces other session layer software with the hardware.

**keyboard send/receive (KSR).** A combination data transmitter and receiver limited to printer receive and keyboard transmit.

**keying.** 1. The modulation of an analog signal to carry digital information. 2. The interruption of a direct current circuit to signal information.

**key management.** The process of managing the keys used for data encryption.

**key telephone set.** A telephone set with push button keys used to provide a variety of services.

**kilobit.** One thousand bits.

**kilohertz.** One thousand hertz, or one thousand cycles per second.

**KSR.** *See* keyboard send/receive.

**ku band.** A popular satellite communications frequency band with a range of 12 to 14 gigahertz.

# L

**LADS.** *See* local area data set.

**LADT.** *See* Local Area Data Transport.

**LAN.** *See* local area network.

**land line.** Any wire connection between any two terrestrial points.

**LAP.** *See* Link Access Protocol.

**LAPD.** *See* Link Access Protocol for the D Channel.

**laser.** Light amplification by stimulated emission. A laser emits light at a single frequency with all radiation "in phase." The emitted light may also be referred to as coherent light.

**LAT.** *See* Local Area Transport.

**LATA.** *See* Local Access and Transport Area.

**late collision.** A failure condition in a CSMA/CD (Carrier Sense Multiple Access with Collision Detection) network.

**latency.** 1. The time between the point at which a station requests access to a network and the point at which such access is granted. 2. The time delay created by the use of any physical device or software process.

**layer.** In the International Standards Organization Open Systems Interconnect (OSI) model, a layer is a collection of functions that represent one level of the hierarchy.

**L band.** A portion of the electromagnetic radiation spectrum used in certain satellite and microwave systems. The frequency used is approximately 1 gigahertz.

**L-carrier system.** A service using a variety of media and occupying a bandwidth from 68 kilohertz to more than 8 million hertz.

**LDM.** *See* limited-distance modem.

**leased line.** A virtual or physical circuit leased from a common carrier for the exclusive use of a specific user. Since the circuit may be virtual, performance may vary from day to day. This service should be compared with a private line, which has a higher cost. Private line facilities will be the same at all times.

## least-cost routing

**least-cost routing.** 1. A private branch exchange service providing least-cost connection to external points. 2. A routing method used at the network layer by some packet-switched networks that directs packets along the least-cost route as defined by a specific algorithm. The algorithm may be defined by a standard or created by a vendor.

**least-significant bit (LSB).** The bit representing the lowest power of 2 (normally 2 raised to the power 0) in a group of bits such as a byte.

**LEC.** *See* local exchange carrier.

**LED.** *See* light-emitting diode.

**LEN.** *See* Low-Entry Networking.

**level 1 relay.** Another name for a repeater. Level 1 indicates that the device operates at the lowest layer (physical layer), as defined by the Open Systems Interconnect (OSI) architecture.

**level 2 relay.** Another name for a bridge. Level 2 indicates that the device operates at the second layer (data link layer), as defined by the Open Systems Interconnect (OSI) architecture.

**level 3 relay.** Another name for a router. Level 3 indicates that the device operates at the third layer (network layer), as defined by the Open Systems Interconnect (OSI) architecture.

**level 7 relay.** Another name for a gateway. Level 7 indicates that the device operates at the seventh layer (application layer) of the Open Systems Interconnect (OSI) architecture.

**LF.** *See* low frequency.

**light-emitting diode (LED).** A solid-state device that radiates light at a single frequency.

**lightwave communication.** A type of communication in which light is used as an information carrier. The term is often used instead of the word "optical" to avoid confusion with other picture transmission systems, such as facsimile.

**limited-distance modem (LDM).** Another term for a short-haul modem.

**line.** A physical path that provides direct communication between devices. In most cases, a line is a length of wire.

**line control.** The process of determining which device is the transmitter and which is the receiver. Line control is handled by the data link control protocol.

**line discipline.** The sequence of operations that results in the actual transmission and reception of data. The set of rules defining the sequence is normally referred to as the communications protocol or data link control protocol.

**line driver.** An electronic device that conditions a digital signal so that it can be transmitted over an extended distance.

**line hit.** A short-term failure of a communications channel's physical medium.

**line-of-sight transmission.** Transmission limited to straight lines. Examples are microwave and laser.

**line turnaround.** In a half-duplex transmission system, the time between when one block of data has been sent and received and the next block can be transmitted. The delay is caused by the fact that the transmit line must be reconfigured to be the receive line, a response from the receiver processed, and the line then reconfigured for transmit before a second block can be sent.

**Link Access Protocol (LAP).** An alternate name for data link control. Link Access Protocol A (LAPA) and Link Access Protocol B (LAPB) are versions of High-Level Data Link Control. CCITT X.25 uses LAPB as its data link control protocol.

**Link Access Protocol for the D Channel (LAPD).** When used in connection with Integrated Services Digital Network (ISDN) technology, LAPD describes the data link layer protocols used in the D channel. It is defined by the CCITT Q.921 recommendation.

**link attached.** Any form of device connection that uses a communications line as opposed to a direct channel connection.

**link redundancy.** The ratio of the actual number of links between nodes in a network and the minimum number that would be required to ensure that any node could transmit to any other node. This ratio is a measure of alternate routing availability.

**LLC.** *See* logical link control.

**load balancing.** The process whereby multiple service units are used equally. For example, if two communications lines are available between two points, each carries half of the traffic load.

**load coil.** A device used to improve a transmission line's communications characteristics.

## loaded line

**loaded line.** A telephone line with induction coils to reduce distortion and increase the transmission speed of the line.

**load host.** A specific device within a network used to download software services to a server node.

**Local Access and Transport Area (LATA).** The local calling areas (area codes) within the U.S. Only regulated long-distance carriers are empowered by the U.S. Federal Communications Commission to provide connection service between LATAs.

**local area data set (LADS).** Another name for a short-haul modem. A LADS is used for data transmission on privately owned wire where the distance exceeds the interface driver specifications. LADSs typically can be used for distances up to ten miles.

**Local Area Data Transport (LADT).** A method developed by AT&T to allow users to transmit data to a central switching office that employs High-Level Data Link Control (HDLC) as its data link control.

**local area network (LAN).** A network in which distances are relatively short, speeds are high, and reliability is excellent.

**Local Area Transport (LAT).** A set of protocols developed by Digital Equipment Corp. to control the transfer of data between a terminal server and its target host using a local area network. LAT has become a *de facto* standard.

**local exchange carrier (LEC).** The local telephone company.

**local loop.** In common carrier (telephone company) voice network terms, the portion of the network between the customer premise and the first switching point (the local office).

**logical link.** A virtual circuit connection between two using entity processes in the same or different computational node.

**logical link control (LLC).** The IEEE local area network description for the equivalent of the International Standards Organization data link control for networks that conform to the Open Systems Interconnect (OSI) architecture. The services provided are reduced to forming a protocol data unit (format for the data). This is then passed to the media access control service provider, which adds both addressing and error detection information before transmission.

**logical unit (LU).** In IBM Corp. Systems Network Architecture terminology, LU refers to a group of upper-level protocols (usually the presentation layer, the session layer, and parts of the transport layer as defined by the OSI Reference Model) and the data formats they produce. With the exception of LU 6.2, these groups of protocols are specific to both physical devices and software environments.

**logic levels.** The voltages, normally between 0.4 and 3.0 volts, that computers use to represent digital states.

**logic signaling levels.** *See* logic levels.

**log in.** *See* log on.

**log on.** To gain access to a system. The log-on process is normally controlled by passwords and user identification codes. In some systems the user identification code is referred to as the PIN, or personal identification number.

**long-haul modem.** A modem designed to operate over distances greater than ten miles and normally in conjunction with telephone company transmission facilities.

**longitudinal parity check (LRC).** A parity check used in conjunction with a vertical redundancy check in parallel data transfers.

**long line driver.** A device used to drive transmission signals up to a few thousand feet.

**loopback.** A method of testing whereby transmitted signals are returned by the receiver or other intermediate devices to the transmitter so that they can be compared with the original data.

**loop resistance.** The total resistance of a wire from one point to another and back.

**loop start.** The most common way of initiating a telephone-based communications session. Removal of the handset from its cradle closes a circuit loop and allows a current to flow, which is then detected by the private branch exchange or local exchange.

**loosely coupled.** A term used by IBM Corp. to describe computers directly connected via their input/output channels.

**loss.** The reduction of transmission signal strength.

**Low-Entry Networking (LEN).** A form of Systems Network Architecture implemented by IBM Corp. to accommodate the networking of System/3x computers.

**low frequency (LF).** Transmission frequencies below 3 megahertz.

**low pass.** The maximum frequency that can be passed through a specific filter. All frequencies below this maximum will be transmitted.

**LRC.** Longitudinal redundancy check.

**LSB.** *See* least-significant bit.

**LU.** *See* logical unit.

**LU 1.** A logical unit that allows for data transfer from an application program to a Systems Network Architecture printer or workstation.

**LU 2.** A logical unit for the transfer of data from an application program to a 3270-type terminal.

**LU 3.** A logical unit for the transfer of data from an application program to a 3270 printer.

**LU 4.** A logical unit for IBM Corp. office products. Host-to-terminal and terminal-to-terminal data transfers can be implemented using LU 4.

**LU 6.** A logical unit for the communication between two programs on the same or different hosts.

**LU 6.2.** A logical unit for program-to-program communications. LU 6.2 is a device-independent set of protocols implemented in personal computers using Advanced Peer-to-Peer Communications/PC software.

**LU 10.** A logical unit similar to LU 6.2 but which allows for specific extensions.

**LUXPAC.** A CCITT X.25 packet-switched network operated in Luxembourg by the Luxembourg government.

# M

**M24.** In T1 digital signaling technology, M24 is a multiplexer that connects 24 DS-0 (64-Kbps) lines to a central office switch.

**M44.** In T1 digital signaling technology, M44 is a multiplexer that connects one T1 line using one form of modulation to two other T1 lines using a different form of modulation.

**MAC.** *See* medium access control.

**mail server.** A computer configured to serve the electronic mail needs of a population of users.

**main.** In telephone terms, a private branch exchange (PBX) or Centrex device into which other PBXs are routed.

**main distribution frame.** In a telephone system, the point at which all subscriber lines are terminated. A main distribution frame may be part of a private branch exchange or, in the case of Centrex service, part of the telephone company's exchange equipment.

**Main Network Address.** An IBM Corp. Systems Network Architecture (SNA) term to describe the logical unit (LU) network address used for LU-to-System Services Control Point (SSCP) sessions.

**Maintenance Operations Protocol (MOP).** A Digital Equipment Corp. Digital Network Architecture (DNA) protocol used in low-level maintenance and testing functions.

**male or female connector.** Connectors are assigned a gender based on whether they provide pins (male) or sockets (female) for attachment.

**MAN.** *See* metropolitan area network.

**Management Event Notification (MEN) Protocol.** An application layer protocol proposed by Digital Equipment Corp. for use in Phase V Digital Network Architecture (DNA). MEN is used for communication between an event source and an event sink, and is part of the protocol suite used for overall network management.

**Management Information Control and Exchange (MICE) Protocol.** An application layer protocol used in Digital Equipment Corp.'s Digital Network Architecture (DNA) Phase V to implement various network management functions.

## Manchester encoding

**Manchester encoding.** A transmission encoding scheme whereby binary ones are represented by positive transitions within a time period, and binary zeros are represented by negative transitions. This scheme is useful in high-speed transmission over short distances and is utilized in DIX Ethernet, IEEE 802.3, and many other baseband local area network implementations.

**Manufacturing Automation Protocol (MAP).** A full seven-layer network architecture designed to operate in industrial environments. The MAP structure conforms to the International Standards Organization (ISO) Open Systems Interconnect (OSI) architecture.

**Manufacturing Message Format Specification (MMFS).** A MAP 2.$n$ application layer protocol that defines the framework for distributing messages throughout a network.

**Manufacturing Message Specification (MMS).** An International Standards Organization (ISO) application layer protocol that defines the framework for distributing manufacturing messages within a network. This specification is used in MAP 3.$n$.

**MAP.** *See* Manufacturing Automation Protocol.

**mapping.** In networking, the logical association of one set of attribute values within one network with a set of attribute values within another network.

**mark.** A transmitted signal to be interpreted as a logical one.

**Mark*net Extended.** A CCITT X.25 packet-switched network operated in the U.S.

**MASER.** *See* microwave amplification by stimulated emission of radiation.

**master clock.** The source of timing for a series of devices, such as nodes, in a network.

**master station.** A station or network node that maintains direct control over other stations or nodes.

**matrix.** An arrangement that allows any input circuit to be connected directly to any output circuit.

**matrix switch.** A device that performs cross-connect switching functions automatically, under program control or under operator control.

**MAU.** *See* medium attachment unit, medium adaptor unit, *and* multistation access unit.

**maximum hops.** A packet-switched network parameter used to limit the number of nodes through which a packet may pass in transit between source and destination. The limit is imposed to prevent the use of long end-to-end routes that consume time and resources.

**Maxnet.** The network architecture used by Modular Computers Inc.

**Maypac.** A CCITT X.25 packet-switched network operated in Malaysia by the central government.

**M bit.** The *more* data bit in an X.25 packet that signifies that a specific message consists of one or more packages yet to be transmitted.

**medium.** Any physical substance used for the transmission of signals.

**medium access control (MAC).** The mechanism whereby devices attached to a local area network gain access to the transmission medium. MAC combines some of the functions of the International Standards Organization Open Systems Interconnect (OSI) data link control layer and the OSI physical layer.

**medium adaptor unit (MAU).** A device used in IBM Corp.'s Token-Ring technology to allow users to create small rings without any interconnecting wire.

**medium attachment unit (MAU).** A device used to attach a processing node to a network at the physical level. An example is the transceiver used to attach devices to an Ethernet cable.

**megabit.** One million bits.

**megabyte.** One "computer million" (1.048576 million) eight-bit bytes.

**megahertz.** One million hertz or one million cycles per second.

**MEN Protocol.** *See* Management Event Notification Protocol.

**message.** A sequence of characters containing the total information that must be transferred from source to destination.

**Message Handling System (MHS).** An International Standards Organization Open Systems Interconnect (OSI) application layer protocol that specifies the framework for distributing data from one network to others. MHS transfers small messages in a store-and-forward manner. MHS is the ISO equivalent to CCITT X.400.

**message number.** A sequential number added to a message to assist in ensuring end-to-end integrity.

**message-switched network**

**message-switched network.** A type of network that chooses routes for each complete message.

**message telephone service (MTS).** The standard designation for long-distance or toll telephone service.

**Message Transfer Agent (MTA).** The software services defined by CCITT X.400 that handle the transfer of messages from source to destination independent of the system hardware or software.

**message unit.** In IBM Corp.'s Systems Network Architecture, the portion of the data within a message that is passed to, and processed by, a specific software layer.

**metropolitan area network (MAN).** A network whose facilities are restricted to individual populated areas. Distances of up to 50 miles are possible, and digital speeds of 1 Mbps to 200 Mbps are typical. Two MAN standards are IEEE 802.6 and ANSI X3T9.5. Cellular telephone systems are implemented in specific metropolitan areas using other CCITT and CCIR standards.

**Metrowave Bridge.** A Digital Equipment Corp. remote bridge supporting a microwave link, which interconnects local area network segments up to five miles apart.

**MHS.** *See* Message Handling System.

**MIA.** *See* Multivendor Integration Architecture.

**MICE Protocol.** *See* Management Information Control and Exchange Protocol.

**Micro Channel architecture (MCA).** The internal bus architecture used in the IBM Corp. Personal System/2 (PS/2) Model 50 and higher.

**Microcom Networking Protocol (MNP).** A protocol defined by Microcom Inc. and used to provide error-free asynchronous transmission. MNP is used extensively to support personal computer integral modems.

**micro-mainframe link.** A connection for data transfer between a microcomputer and a mainframe established using a combination of hardware and software.

**microwave.** Radio transmission in the high gigahertz range. Microwave is used heavily for data transmission over short distances, from 20 to 40 miles.

**microwave amplification by stimulated emission of radiation (MASER).** A special-purpose microwave amplification technique used extensively in satellite ground stations to amplify the signal received from space.

**microwave pulse generator (MPG).** A device that generates pulses at microwave frequencies.

**MIF.** *See* minimum internetworking functionality.

**Millar coding.** A transmission encoding method sometimes used for baseband transmission over telephone company twisted-pair wire.

**MIL-STD-1777.** Internet Protocol (IP). A U.S. Department of Defense specification corresponding to the ISO 8472 protocol providing for connectionless network service.

**MIL-STD-1778.** Transmission Control Protocol (TCP). A U.S. Department of Defense specification corresponding to the ISO 8073 connection-oriented transport protocol.

**MIL-STD-1780.** File Transfer Protocol (FTP). A U.S. Department of Defense specification corresponding to the ISO 8571 file transfer and access method.

**MIL-STD-1781.** Simple Mail Transfer Protocol (SMTP). A U.S. Department of Defense specification corresponding to the CCITT X.400 Message Handling System (MHS).

**MIL-STD-1782.** TELNET Protocol. A U.S. Department of Defense specification corresponding to the ISO 9041 Virtual Terminal Protocol.

**Mini-MAP.** An implementation of the Manufacturing Automation Protocol that allows for standardization of only the application and physical levels. Mini-MAP is intended to provide a low-cost approach to process-control networking.

**minimum internetworking functionality (MIF).** An International Standards Organization (ISO) definition of the basic functions of a local area network node that is capable of connecting to a wide area network.

**MMFS.** *See* Manufacturing Message Format Specification.

**MMS.** *See* Manufacturing Message Specification.

**MNP.** *See* Microcom Networking Protocol.

**modem.** A device used to process a digital signal so that it can be transmitted on an analog transmission line. The word is derived from a contraction of the words "modulator" and "demodulator." Modems may use amplitude, frequency, or phase shift modulation.

**modem eliminator.** A device connecting a terminal, for example, to a local computer, eliminating the need for a modem where one is required by the specific hardware or software. May also be called a null modem.

**modem-sharing device.** A device that allows more than one transmitting unit to use the same modem.

**modulation.** The process whereby a transmission signal is modified to carry some type of information.

**modulation rate.** The reciprocal of the time interval between the shortest significant events, such as encoding bits, occurring in a modulated signal. If the measure is expressed in seconds, the rate is given in baud.

**modulo-n. 1.** The quantity of messages or frames that can be counted before the counter is reset to zero. **2.** The number of messages, $n$-1, that can be sent by a transmitter before an acknowledgment must be received from the receiver.

**monitor. 1.** Hardware or software that receives network performance and operation information for record keeping or decision making. **2.** Another name for a cathode ray tube (CRT) or video display unit (VDU)-type terminal.

**MOP.** *See* Maintenance Operations Protocol.

**MPG.** *See* microwave pulse generator.

**MS-DOS.** The popular disk-based operating system developed by Microsoft Corp. to control the operation of the IBM Corp. PC XT, PC AT, and certain Personal System/2 models.

**MS LAN Manager.** A local area network implementation and control approach and supporting software products developed jointly by 3Com Corp. and Microsoft Corp. that includes a definition of the network architecture and software modules needed for operation. MS LAN Manager software provides several network control functions not normally available with PC network software.

**MSNF.** *See* Multisystem Networking Facility.

**MTA.** *See* Message Transfer Agent.

**MTS.** *See* message telephone service.

## multipoint

**multiaccess connection.** A connection method whereby any attached station can transmit to any number of other stations. The most popular example is used by the bus topology used in the IEEE 802.3/ Ethernet implementation.

**multidomain network.** In IBM Corp. Systems Network Architecture technology, a network that contains more than one host-based System Services Control Point (SSCP).

**multidrop.** A type of connection whereby transmission from one device can be directed to a successive series of devices.

**multileaving.** The process of transmitting more than one data stream on the same communications channel at the same time.

**multimode fiber.** A fiber-optic transmission element designed to carry more than one frequency at the same time.

**multinode network.** In T1 digital signaling technology, a network that has more than one switch working in tandem with other geographically separated switches.

**multiple address message.** A message addressed to two or more destination points.

**multiple line controller.** A hardware device that can control the transmit or receive functions of two or more transmission lines simultaneously. Such functions include direction (transmit or receive) and timing (synchronous or asynchronous).

**multiple routing.** The process whereby a single message is sent to more than one destination via the same or different routes.

**Multiple Virtual Storage (MVS).** A common IBM Corp. mainframe operating system which optimizes online, real-time, multiuser, multitasking operation.

**multiplexer (MUX).** A device that merges multiple low-speed data streams onto a single high-speed line.

**multiplexing. 1.** The process whereby more than one low-speed communications device uses one high-speed transmission line. **2.** The process whereby any number of entities can be made to use a single entity.

**multipoint.** A type of connection whereby transmission from one primary point can be directed to any of several secondary points.

**multiport repeater.** A repeater that collects signals from one transmission channel and, after performing the standard repeater functions, retransmits the signals to more than one new transmission channel.

**multiport transceiver.** A transceiver that allows a number of devices to be attached to one local area network transceiver attachment on the backbone network.

**multistation access unit (MAU).** A wiring concentrator used in local area networks.

**Multisystem Networking Facility (MSNF).** An IBM Corp. communications facility implemented in software that allows more than one host based on the IBM 5370 architecture to control the configuration and performance of a network.

**Multivendor Integration Architecture (MIA).** An architecture for the interconnection of multivendor systems proposed by Nippon Telegraph and Telephone (NTT) of Tokyo. The proposal is significant because NTT is considered one of the world's largest communications companies.

**MUX.** *See* multiplexer.

**MVS.** *See* Multiple Virtual Storage.

**MVS Enterprise System Architecture (MVS/ESA).** A version of IBM Corp.'s Systems Network Architecture (SNA) centered around the 309x series of mainframes.

**MVS/ESA.** *See* MVS Enterprise System Architecture.

# N

**NAK.** *See* not acknowledge character.

**nanosecond.** One billionth of a second.

**NAPLSP.** *See* National American Presentation Level Syntax Protocol.

**narrowband.** A transmission channel whose bandwidth (frequency range) is lower than that of a typical voice channel.

**NARUC.** *See* National Association of Regulatory Utility Commissioners.

**n-ary code.** A code used to encode real-world characters that use *n* different code elements. Examples are binary (two states) and tertiary (three states).

**NAS.** *See* Network Application Support.

**National American Presentation Level Syntax Protocol (NAPLSP).** A presentation-level specification for representing graphics information in the form of ASCII text.

**National Association of Regulatory Utility Commissioners (NARUC).** An organization supporting the needs of the commissioners of U.S. federal and state regulatory agencies.

**National Bureau of Standards (NBS).** The U.S. government organization that helps prepare non-Department of Defense communications standards and operates a testing service to indicate conformity to existing standards. *Address*: Institute for Computer Sciences and Technology, National Bureau of Standards, Gaithersburg, MD 20899.

**National Cable Television Association (NCTA).** An organization representing the major U.S. cable television operators.

**National Exchange Carrier Association (NECA).** An association of local exchange carriers mandated by the U.S. Federal Communications Commission upon the divestiture of AT&T.

**National Institute for Standards and Technology (NIST).** The U.S. government agency that oversees the operation of the U.S. National Bureau of Standards. The NIST is based in Gaithersburg, MD.

**National Science Foundation Network (NSFNET).** The National Science Foundation Network currently connects several universities and operates at the T1 rate of 1.544 Mbps.

**National Telecommunications and Information Administration (NTIA).** A group within the U.S. Department of Commerce concerned with the development of communications standards.

## National Television System Committee (NTSC)

**National Television System Committee (NTSC).** The NTSC specification for the transmitted signal in television broadcasting in the U.S. is a *de facto* standard.

**native mode.** The use of a communications protocol in the environment for which it was developed or optimized.

**NAU.** *See* Network Addressable Unit.

**NBS.** *See* National Bureau of Standards.

**NCC.** *See* Network Control Center.

**NCCF.** *See* Network Communications Control Facility.

**NCL.** *See* Network Control Language.

**NCP.** *See* Network Control Program *and* Network Control Protocol.

**NCTA.** *See* National Cable Television Association.

**NCTE.** *See* Network Channel Terminating Equipment.

**NDT.** *See* net data throughput.

**near-end crosstalk (NEXT).** The transfer of energy, normally observed as transmission noise, between circuits at the source (near) end of a transmission link.

**near instantaneous companding (NIC).** The very fast quantizing of an analog signal into digital representation.

**NECA.** *See* National Exchange Carrier Association.

**NetBios.** *See* Network Basic Input/Output System.

**net data throughput (NDT).** The rate at which data is transferred on a communications channel, normally specified in bits per second.

**NetView.** An IBM Corp. software product that allows for the control of complex networks such as those consisting of both traditional Systems Network Architecture (SNA) implementations and local area networks. NetView can operate only in connection with network products specified by IBM.

**NetWare.** A local area network implementation and control approach developed by Novell Inc. that defines the network architecture and the software modules needed for network operations. NetWare is also the name of the network software.

## Network Control Program (NCP)

**network.** A group of devices interconnected using a method or architecture that eliminates the need to have every device directly connected to every other device.

**Network Addressable Unit (NAU).** In IBM Corp.'s Systems Network Architecture, an entity which is the source or the destination of an information transfer session.

**network application architecture.** A generalized architecture allowing interoperability at the application level. Examples are Digital Equipment Corp.'s Network Application Support (NAS) and IBM Corp.'s Systems Application Architecture (SAA).

**Network Application Support (NAS).** The environment defined by Digital Equipment Corp. to provide integration of services at the application level by using industry-standard services and interfaces.

**network architecture.** The procedures and rules used to design, build, implement, and operate a network of interconnected devices.

**Network Basic Input/Output System (NetBios).** Within the context of the MS-DOS operating system, the software or software and firmware services that implement the interface between applications and a network adaptor, such as a CSMA/CD or token-ring adaptor.

**Network Channel Terminating Equipment (NCTE).** Equipment considered necessary for the proper termination of telephone company facilities at a customer's premises. The Carterphone ruling by the U.S. Federal Communications Commission made it possible for third parties to supply this equipment.

**Network Communications Control Facility (NCCF).** A set of IBM Corp. software routines used for monitoring and controlling network functions and operations.

**Network Control Center (NCC).** A physical point within a network where various management and control functions are implemented.

**Network Control Language (NCL).** A command line interface language used by Digital Equipment Corp.'s Digital Network Architecture (DNA).

**Network Control Program (NCP).** An IBM Corp. Systems Network Architecture term. This is the program that switches the virtual circuit connections into place, implements path control, and operates the Synchronous Data Link Control (SDLC) link. The Network Control Program is normally resident in the communications controller or the host processor.

## Network Control Protocol

**Network Control Protocol.** The original transport layer protocol used in ARPANET, later replaced by Transmission Control Protocol.

**network diameter.** The length of the shortest path between the two most physically separated nodes within a network.

**Network File System (NFS).** A method developed by Sun Microsystems Inc. for distributing files within a heterogenous network. NFS has become a *de facto* standard. It requires special software drivers to suit specific vendor hardware and operating system software. NFS hardware and software gateway products are also available.

**Network Information and Control Exchange (NICE).** A high level set of software services in Digital Equipment Corp.'s DECnet that performs downline loading of data or software and upline dumping of data.

**network interface.** The interface between a network and a computational device. An example is an Ethernet or IEEE 802.3 controller, which interfaces a specific computer or other device to an Ethernet or IEEE 802.3 local area network.

**network layer.** The layer in a layered network architecture responsible for choosing routes or circuits for transmission and packet-switching decisions. Examples are CCITT X.25, Xerox Corp.'s Xerox Network Services (XNS) network layer, Digital Equipment Corp.'s Routing Protocol, and IBM Corp.'s Path Control.

**network management software.** The software that manages and controls all network functions within a network.

**network object.** Any specific entity that can be manipulated by a set of defined operations. Devices, databases, programs, and processors can all be defined as network objects.

**network operating system (NOS).** The software components that allow a computer to participate in network applications.

**network operations center.** The physical location from which the operational functions of a network are controlled. May also be called network control center.

**Network Problem Determination Application (NPDA).** An IBM Corp. program that aids operators in finding network problems from a single point.

**network protocol analyzer.** A device designed to monitor the functions of individual protocols or multiple protocols in complete networks and provide performance and maintenance data.

**network protocol data unit (NPDU).** The form into which the network layer of the Open Systems Interconnect (OSI) network architecture formats data for use and recognition.

**network redundancy.** In a network, the state of having more connecting links than the minimum required to provide a connecting path between all nodes.

**network relay.** Another name for a router.

**network service access point (NASP).** A logical, addressable point at which network services are made available to requesting user entities. The NASP is a specific interface consideration of the network layer in a layered network architecture.

**network services.** 1. Any set of software services that facilitate network operation. 2. In IBM Corp. Systems Network Architecture technology, the services within Network Addressable Units that control network operations.

**Network Termination 1 (NT1).** In Integrated Services Digital Network (ISDN) technology, the device that terminates the actual T1 transmission line at the physical level.

**Network Termination 2 (NT2).** In Integrated Services Digital Network (ISDN) technology, a device that performs the customer premises switching or multiplexing function.

**network topology.** The physical relationships between devices in a network. An example is the ring topology, in which all devices are connected in a physical ring.

**network traffic.** The total amount of data transferred over a network at some period in time.

**network virtual terminal.** A process whereby a network accommodates terminal devices with different characteristics by converting the varying characteristics into a single format so that all terminals appear the same.

**NETWORTH.** The Canadian equivalent of the worldwide BITNET. NETWORTH connects universities and other institutions of higher learning.

**NEXT.** *See* near-end crosstalk.

**NFS.** *See* Network File System.

**NFSNET.** *See* National Science Foundation Network.

## NIC

**NIC.** *See* near instantaneous companding.

**NICE.** *See* Network Information and Control Exchange.

**NIST.** *See* National Institute of Standards and Technology.

**nodal processor.** In T1 digital transmission technology, nodal processor is often used instead of the word "multiplexer."

**node.** A computational or switching point within a network.

**node address.** The unique identifier used to describe a specific node.

**node name.** A user-defined name for a node within a network. This name will normally have to be translated into a system address at the start of a transfer session.

**node visit count.** A method of eliminating looping between nodes whereby the transmitting device specifies the maximum number of nodes that can be "visited" during transmission. If this number is exceeded and the final destination has not been reached, the package is discarded. Node visit counts are used in the network layer of some packet-switching networks as well as in Digital Equipment Corp.'s DECnet Phase IV.

**noise.** Portions of a signal in a transmission medium that are the result of external influences and are not part of the original transmission.

**noise suppressor.** A device used in conjunction with, or built into, a receiver to reduce or eliminate transmission noise.

**nonadaptive routing.** A routing method that cannot adapt to or accommodate changes in a network.

**nonblocking switch.** A switching system where a connection path always exists for each attached device.

**noninteractive system.** A system in which no interaction occurs between a user and a computer during the execution of a computer program.

**non-return to zero (NRZ).** A transmission encoding scheme whereby two separate states are used to define binary ones and zeros. Neither state is the electrical zero.

**non-return to zero inverted (NRZI).** A transmission encoding scheme where binary zeros change the signal state and binary ones do not. Neither state is the electrical zero.

**nonrouting node.** A network node that cannot perform routing functions. May also be called an end node.

## null suppression

**nonswitched line.** A permanent transmission link between two devices. This type of connection may also be referred to as a hard-wired connection.

**nontransparent mode.** A transmission mode whereby decisions about what is data and what is control information cannot be made until all of a transmission unit, such as a block, has been received.

**NOS.** *See* network operating system.

**not acknowledge character (NAK).** The encoded character used to indicate that transmitted data has been received but errors have been detected.

**NPDA.** *See* Network Problem Determination Application.

**NPDU.** *See* network protocol data unit.

**NRZ.** *See* non-return to zero.

**NRZI.** *See* non-return to zero inverted.

**NSAP.** *See* network service access point.

**NSFNET.** *See* National Science Foundation Network.

**NSP.** The set of protocols used at the transport layer in Digital Equipment Corp.'s implementation of the Digital Network Architecture (DNA).

**NT1.** *See* Network Termination 1.

**NT2.** *See* Network Termination 2.

**NTIA.** *See* National Telecommunications and Information Administration.

**NTSC.** *See* National Television System Committee.

**null.** Having no value.

**null characters.** Characters that can be added to a data stream without altering its information content. Null characters are used to satisfy timing requirements or to fill out unused but necessary portions of message fields.

**null modem.** A device that connects two terminals or computers by emulating the characteristics of a modem. Similar to a modem eliminator.

**null suppression.** A data compression technique whereby streams of null characters are identified at a transmission source and replaced by two or more control characters. The first character indicates the null suppression, and more characters indicate the number of null characters removed. The receiver uses this information to replace the removed data.

**Nyquist theorem**

**Nyquist theorem.** A formula stating that two samples per cycle of a specific analog bandwidth signal are sufficient to characterize it.

# O

**OC-1.** The optical interface designed to work with the STS-1 signaling rate in a Synchronous Optical Network (SONET).

**OC-n.** The optical interface designed to work with the STS-n signaling rate in a Synchronous Optical Network (SONET). Currently, *n* is an integer between 1 and 48.

**OCR.** *See* optical character recognition.

**octet.** A set of eight bits. The term "octect" is favored by the CCITT and used in place of the more common term "byte."

**odd parity.** An error-checking process whereby the transmitted characters have been forced by the transmitter to always have an odd numeric value.

**off hook.** The state indicating that a telephone circuit is available for use.

**office.** A physical routing point and its associated hardware devices and software facilities.

**office class.** The definition of a telephone switching and routing facility within the transmission hierarchy. An example is toll office, which is the switch that routes signals from a local office to the long-distance connections.

**offline.** The state of a device not connected to a computer. The functions of an offline device cannot be under the control of a central processing unit.

**off-load.** To remove network overhead from a specific node.

**ONA.** *See* Open Network Architecture.

**ones density.** The characteristic of a public digital network that requires that no data stream consist of more than seven zeros in a row. This limitation ensures proper timing. Several control algorithms are used (for example, one-bit insertion) to prevent the appearance of eight or more consecutive zeros.

**on Ethernet cache.** A term used by Digital Equipment Corp. to describe the memory spaces used by Ethernet nodes to store device addresses for machines on the same network.

**one-way trunk.** A line between a private branch exchange and a central office, or between two central offices where communication proceeds in one direction only.

**on hook.** The normal, inactive condition of a telephone system terminal device.

## online

**online.** The state of a device connected directly to a computer and hence under the ongoing control of a central processing unit.

**open-air transmission.** Transmission that does not require a closed transmission medium, such as wire or fiber. May also be referred to as noncontained transmission.

**Open Network Architecture (ONA).** A network architecture defined by the U.S. Federal Communications Commission to allow regional Bell operating companies to market add-on services in a network environment. ONA services include transaction processing, Videotex, and voice messaging.

**open shortest path first (OSPF).** A routing protocol proposed by a number of intermediate-level interconnection device vendors. The proposed technique routes packages by finding the shortest path available to the destination.

**Open Systems Interconnect (OSI).** A seven-layer model developed by the International Standards Organization (ISO). The model defines a set of software and hardware functions used to implement the connection of systems and facilitate the transfer of data between them.

**OpenView.** The network management architecture developed and used by Hewlett-Packard Co.

**Operating System/2 (OS/2).** The operating system developed by IBM Corp. for the Personal System/2 series of computers.

**operating system (OS).** Software that manages a system's internal and external resources. Most aspects of networking are implemented using facilities provided by a specific operating system.

**Operating System/Virtual Storage (OS/VS).** A popular IBM Corp. mainframe operating system.

**optical character recognition (OCR).** A process whereby text characters are recognized using a light-based system and translated into computer characters such as ASCII.

**optical fiber.** Any glass or plastic fiber manufactured for the transmission of light signals.

**originate/answer.** The two modes of operation for a modem. Originate and answer states define the frequencies used to transmit and receive. In a two-way communication system, one modem must be set to originate and one to answer.

**OS.** *See* operating system.

**OS/2.** *See* Operating System/2.

**OSAK.** *See* OSI Session Application Kernel.

**oscillator.** A device used to generate analog signals at a specific amplitude and frequency and in the form of a sine wave. The signal generated is then used as the carrier of information between source and destination.

**OSI.** *See* Open Systems Interconnect.

**OSInet.** A test network used by the U.S. National Bureau of Standards to test vendor product conformance to OSI standards and specifications.

**OSI Network Management Forum.** A consortium of more than 100 equipment vendors and carriers working on the development of specifications to support the Open Systems Interconnect (OSI) network management effort.

**OSI Network Management (OSI/NM).** The International Standards Organization (ISO) proposed network management services. Network management software normally allows for the control, monitoring and change of all network functions. The services are currently defined in the form of draft proposals, which after review and possible modification, will become ISO standards.

**OSI/NM.** *See* OSI Network Management.

**OSI Reference Model.** The seven-layer architecture recommended by the International Standards Organization (ISO) for computer interconnection. The seven layers are collectively referred to as the Reference Model for Open Systems Interconnect (OSI).

**OSI Session Application Kernel (OSAK).** A Digital Equipment Corp. software product that modifies the DECnet session layer to conform to the Open Systems Interconnect (OSI) session layer as defined by the International Standards Organization.

**OSPF.** *See* open shortest path first.

**OS/VS.** *See* Operating System/Virtual Storage.

**other common carrier.** A regulated common carrier that was not part of the original Bell family of companies.

**outage.** The condition that occurs when a line or circuit is unable to provide a clear transmission path because of disconnection, excessive noise, and so forth.

**outgoing access**

**outgoing access.** A CCITT description of the ability of a device in one network to communicate with a device in another network.

**overhead.** A general term describing all of the data transmitted during an information transfer that is not part of the actual information.

**overhead bit.** A bit having no informational value, normally a controlling bit.

**override.** The process whereby a device seizes a circuit or line for its own use even if the circuit or line is in use by another device.

**overrun.** The fault condition whereby a receiving device loses data because of its inability to accept data at the rate that it is transmitted.

# P

**pacing group.** In IBM Corp.'s Systems Network Architecture, the number of transmission frames that can be sent without a response.

**packet.** A predefined unit of data that is moved from source to destination through a packet-switched network. Types of packets include Transmission Control Protocol/Internet Protocol (TCP/IP) packets used in UNIX systems, Network Services Protocol (NSP) packets used in Digital Equipment Corp. networks, and Internetwork Packet Exchange (IPX) and Sequential Packet Exchange (SPX) packets used in Novell Inc. NetWare networks.

**packet assembler/disassembler (PAD).** A device that creates packets from streams of data elements so that they can be transmitted through a packet-switched network and then replaces them in their original form at the final receiving point. PADs used with an X.25 network conform to the CCITT X.3 specification.

**packet buffer.** A small memory space used to store packets before, during, and after transmission.

**packetized voice.** A form of digital voice transmission that utilizes discrete packets of information. Packetized voice is useful in T1 transmission systems and Integrated Services Digital Network (ISDN) transmission.

**packet-mode terminal.** A terminal device that can receive and transmit data packets over a packet-switched network.

**packet-switched data network (PSDN).** A network in which data is transmitted and routed in specified groupings called packets. CCITT X.25 specifications define the format and procedures for the major public packet-switched data networks in operation.

**packet-switched exchange (PSE).** In CCITT X.25 packet-switched networks, an intermediate switching point or node.

**packet-switched network.** A network in which routing is chosen for individual portions of a message, called packets. The route each packet follows during transmission may or may not be the same route taken by the previous packet. At each point in the network, the next part of the route is chosen on the basis of a particular algorithm.

**PACNET.** A packet-switched network implemented in Taiwan and operated by the Taiwanese government.

**PAD. 1.** A passive network that reduces the power level of a signal without introducing distortion. **2.** *See* packet assembler/disassembler *and* PAD character.

## PAD character

**PAD character.** 1. A transmission control character used to fill space allocated to data in a frame when no data exists. PAD characters are used by IBM Corp.'s Binary Synchronous Communications (BSC) protocol. 2. Any character used to occupy space that is normally occupied by data elements.

**PAM.** *See* pulse amplitude modulation.

**P/AR.** *See* peak-to-average ratio.

**PAR.** *See* positive acknowledgment retransmit.

**parallel interface.** The interface between a device, such as a computer or terminal, and the multiple transmission channels needed to support parallel transmission.

**parallel-to-serial conversion.** The process whereby parallel data carried on a computer's internal bus system is converted into a serial stream for transmission.

**parallel transmission.** The process whereby binary bits are transmitted in groups of 8, 16 or 32 bits requiring the appropriate number of conductors. Parallel transmission is typically used to transfer data to high-speed peripherals such as printers or disks.

**parity bit.** The bit added to an encoded character to force the total sum of the bits to be either odd or even.

**parity check.** The process whereby a single bit is added to an encoded character by the transmitting device to force the total sum of the bits to always be odd (odd parity) or even (even parity). To check for errors, the receiver can check the oddness or evenness of the received value.

**passive side.** When describing a loopback test, passive side is used to identify the device that sends back the transmitted messages for testing.

**passive star.** A type of ring topology in which groups of connections are made via wiring boxes, giving the appearance of a star configuration. Passive star topologies are implemented to allow devices to be added to a ring without halting the ring's operation.

**pass through.** The process of accessing one device via another device. The intermediate device performs the pass-through function.

**pass window.** The range of frequencies used in a transmission system to transmit voice or data signals. More often referred to as bandwidth.

**path.** Any possible route within a network.

**path control.** IBM Corp.'s implementation of what is normally referred to as the network layer in the International Standards Organization Open Systems Interconnect (OSI) layered network architecture.

**path cost.** The cost of a specific network path in terms of vendor-fixed units or user-established criteria.

**path length.** The logical length of a connection path as opposed to the physical length. The path length is described in terms of the number of hops from device to device in the path between the source and destination.

**Pathworks.** The software suite, including service and utility modules, developed by Digital Equipment Corp. to implement its Personal Computer Systems Architecture (PCSA). This software suite has had two name changes. Originally called PCSA, the suite's name was changed to LANworks, then Pathworks.

**PBX.** *See* private branch exchange.

**PC.** *See* personal computer.

**PCM.** *See* pulse code modulation.

**PCSA.** *See* Personal Computer Systems Architecture.

**PDM.** *See* pulse duration modulation.

**PDN.** *See* public data network.

**PDU.** *See* protocol data unit.

**peak-to-average ratio (P/AR).** A measure of the quality of analog transmission lines favored by the Bell system. The P/AR test consists of transmitting signals at a number of frequencies and amplitudes and comparing the received signals with the transmitted signals.

**peak traffic.** The maximum traffic flow in data bits or characters per unit time in a predefined period of time. An example is the maximum data rate in characters per second in any 24-hour period.

**peer protocol.** The set of rules defining the procedures for communication between like entities. The identical entities may be devices or software modules at specific layers in a layered network architecture implementation.

**penetration tap.** A connection method used in Ethernet installations that allows devices to be connected to the cable without interrupting network operation. A sharp, pointed probe is used to penetrate the outer insulation and grounding shield of the coaxial cable and to make direct contact with the inner conductor.

**permanent virtual circuit (PVC)**

**permanent virtual circuit (PVC).** 1. A permanent virtual connection established between two entities at service subscription time. 2. A CCITT X.25 term used to describe a packet-switched service similar in function to a dedicated line.

**persistence.** The probability that when a device on a local area network which has the data to transmit senses a free transmission line it will attempt the transmission. 1.0 persistence indicates that there is 100 percent probability that the device will always attempt to transmit. IEEE 802.3 and Ethernet both use 1.0 persistence. A 0.5 persistence indicates that when a device senses a free line it will only attempt to transmit 50 percent of the time.

**personal computer (PC).** A computer engineered to satisfy the needs of an individual.

**Personal Computer Systems Architecture (PCSA).** A network architecture defined and supported by Digital Equipment Corp. for the incorporation of personal computers into server-based networks.

**personal identification number (PIN).** A number assigned to the user of a specific service and used by controlling systems to validate access to that service. May also be referred to as user identification number or user ID.

**phase.** The relative timing of an alternating signal.

**phase hit.** In telephone terms, the unwanted and significant change in the phase of a modulated analog signal caused by external factors.

**phase jitter.** The unwanted shortening or lengthening of cycles in an analog signal resulting in distortion and possible error.

**phaselock loop.** An electronic circuit used as a phase detector.

**phase roll.** Variations in the phase of a transmitted signal and its echoed-back modem verification. Phase roll is encountered most often in international systems.

**phase shift keying (PSK).** An alternate term for phase shift modulation. Phase shift keying is an early telegraph term based on physical key operation.

**phase shift modulation.** The process whereby the phase angle of an analog signal is varied to carry digital information. It is the most popular modulation method used by common carriers in high-speed data transmission systems.

**physical address.** A set of numbers (or some other unique identifier) that denotes a specific piece of hardware.

**physical layer.** The layer in a layered network architecture, such as the International Standards Organization's Open Systems Interconnect (OSI) seven-layer model, that is responsible for the transmission of bits across the medium. Typical specifications include RS 232-C and the physical layer signaling specified in IEEE 802.3. May also be referred to as the physical level.

**physical layer signaling (PLS).** The electrical process of transferring information from a transmission interface to the communications channel. PLS is treated as a sublayer in IEEE local area network standards.

**physical level relay.** Another name for a repeater.

**physical link.** A hardware-established communications path.

**physical medium attachment (PMA).** A device used to physically attach a node to a network cable. The term is used heavily in local area network environments. An Ethernet transceiver is a good example of a PMA.

**physical unit (PU).** An IBM Corp. Systems Network Architecture term that refers to specific types of IBM hardware that can be interconnected based on a precise set of rules.

**piggybacking.** A technique used at the data link or transport layer in a layered network architecture that allows for transmission acknowledgments to be carried in transmission frames received from the destination.

**PIN.** *See* personal identification number *and* positive, intrinsic, negative.

**ping.** A network management procedure used to determine the status of a "TCP" (Transmission Control Protocol) Internet device.

**pipelining.** A technique used at the transport layer or data link layer in a layered network architecture that allows for the transmission of multiple frames without waiting to see if they are acknowledged on an individual basis. Each frame may have to be acknowledged later and in sequence, or a process of implied acknowledgment may be employed. Implied acknowledgment is a process whereby negative acknowledgment of a specific frame implies that all previously transmitted frames have been received correctly.

**plastic optic fiber (POF).** A fiber transmission medium fabricated from a plastic material. Such a medium uses low-quality light sources and can carry data at speeds greater than 10 Mbps over distances up to 100 meters. POF is evolving as a replacement for twisted-pair wire.

**PLS.** *See* physical layer signaling.

**PMA.** *See* physical medium attachment.

**PMR.** *See* poor man's routing.

**POF.** *See* plastic optic fiber.

**point of presence (POP).** The point of access to a long-distance carrier from within a local telephone network.

**point-of-sale (POS) terminal.** A device located at a retail point of sale and connected to a remote computer. The POS terminal is designed to process limited transactions and receive and transmit data.

**point-to-point connection.** A direct communications link connecting two systems.

**Point-to-Point Protocol (PPP).** An Internet protocol defined by RFC 1172 and 1171 and used to control the transfer of Transmission Control Protocol/Internet Protocol (TCP/IP) packets across dedicated serial transmission lines.

**polarity.** One of two possible states, such as positive and negative, for voltage, charge, current, and so forth.

**polarization.** A property of electromagnetic radiation defining the relationship of the signal vector to the direction of the wave front.

**poll.** The technique by which devices or communications channels are sequentially checked for data or transmission activity.

**polling delay.** The interval between subsequent polls of a device or transmission line.

**poor man's routing (PMR).** A technique used in many packet-switched networks to allow a source node to predefine the routing to the destination, bypassing the normal routing algorithm implemented at the network layer.

**POP.** *See* point of presence.

**port.** An interface of a computer or other transmission device that acts as an input or output point or both.

**POS.** *See* point-of-sale terminal.

**positive acknowledgment retransmit (PAR).** A general group of control protocols under whose control devices acknowledge receipt of correctly received data and require retransmission of data received in error.

**positive, intrinsic, negative (PIN).** A type of photo detector used in fiber-optic transmission.

**POSIX.** Portable Operating System Interface, UNIX. A proposed universal UNIX interface to user-created application programs that would run on all vendor equipment, thereby improving system interoperability.

**Post, Telephone and Telegraph (PTT) Administration.** A national regulatory agency that oversees telecommunications activity. PTTs are common in Europe.

**power line carrier system.** A local area network technique that utilizes a building's existing power distribution cables, such as 110-volt, 60-cycle cables, eliminating the need for special cable installation.

**PPM.** *See* pulse position modulation.

**preamble.** A pattern of bits transmitted at the start of a transmission frame used to implement transmitter and receiver synchronization.

**presentation layer.** The layer of the Open Systems Interconnect (OSI) architecture governing such services as code translation, encryption, and forms management. The presentation layer governs the format in which data is transferred to the session layer in the transmitting system and received from the session layer at the receiving system. May also be referred to as the presentation level.

**Prestel.** A Videotex service offered by British Telecom in the U.K.

**PRI.** *See* Primary Rate Interface.

**primary buffer.** Memory set aside for the storing of data during transmission or reception.

**Primary Rate Interface (PRI).** In Integrated Services Digital Network (ISDN) technology, the interface used to connect a private branch exchange, for example, to the transmission network. In the U.S., the interface connects 23 64-Kbps B channels and one 64-Kbps D channel.

**primary station.** Any node in a network that controls the flow of information on an interconnecting link.

**primitives.** The set of basic signals from which a transfer control protocol can be constructed or the set of symbols from which all designs are constructed in a graphics system.

**printer server.** A local area network node that services the printing needs of other nodes. May also be referred to as a print server.

**private branch exchange (PBX).** The switching point controlling the connection and transfer between all internal telephone extensions and between any internal extension and external trunks.

**Professional Office System (PROFS).** IBM Corp. office automation software that runs on IBM System/370 mainframes.

**PROFS.** *See* Professional Office System.

**programmable read-only memory (PROM).** A type of memory device that can be written to once and then read but not subsequently changed.

**programmable terminal.** A terminal device that has computational capability. May also be called an intelligent terminal.

**programmed I/O.** The transfer of data from or to an input or output device controller under program control. Programmed I/O is normally implemented using device interrupts.

**program-to-program communication.** The process whereby programs running on different computers use certain software facilities to interact directly. This type of communication normally is implemented as a set of higher-level protocols in a layered network architecture.

**PROM.** *See* programmable read-only memory.

**propagation delay.** The delay caused by the finite speed at which electronic signals can travel through a transmission medium. Propagation delay is estimated at 160,000,000 meters per second in copper wire. *Note:* No signal can travel through any medium faster than the speed of light, which is 300,000,000 meters per second, or 186,000 miles per second.

**propagation velocity.** The speed at which electrons or photons travel through a transmission medium.

**protocol.** A collection of rules implemented to execute and control a specific process.

**protocol converter.** A device that converts one set of transmission control rules into another. For example, a protocol converter might receive data according to the High-Level Data Link Control (HDLC) set of rules but retransmit it according to Synchronous Data Link Control (SDLC).

**protocol data unit (PDU).** 1. The form in which data must appear as defined by a specific protocol. 2. The format of data delivered to the media access control layer in a local area network conforming to one of the IEEE standards.

**protocol family.** Any set of communications protocols that use the same addressing mechanism. May also be referred to as an address family.

**protocol filtering.** The process whereby a communications device is programmed to filter out transmissions that use predefined high-level protocols. This facility is useful in bridges and routers connecting systems in multivendor environments.

**protocol stacks.** Groups of protocols that normally are implemented and operated together and that cannot be broken down for conversion. Also called protocol suites.

**protocol suites.** *See* protocol stacks.

**PSDN.** *See* packet-switched data network.

**PSDS.** *See* public switched digital service.

**PSE.** *See* packet-switched exchange.

**pseudo-random bit pattern.** A test pattern of either 511 or 2,047 bits arranged to include all possible bit combinations and used to test network facilities.

**PSK.** *See* phase shift keying.

**PSM.** *See* phase shift modulation.

**PSS.** A packet-switched network implemented in the U.K. by one of the privately owned common carriers.

**PSTN.** *See* public switched telephone network.

**PTN-1.** A CCITT X.25 packet-switched network operated in the U.S.

**PTT.** *See* Post, Telephone and Telegraph Administration.

**PU.** *See* physical unit.

**PU 1.** Physical Unit Type 1. An IBM Corp. Systems Network Architecture (SNA) designation indicating a pre-SNA terminal, such as an IBM 3270 terminal.

**PU 2.** Physical Unit Type 2. An IBM Corp. Systems Network Architecture (SNA) designator specifying a cluster terminal controller such as a 3274 controller.

**PU 2.1.** An IBM Corp. Systems Network Architecture (SNA) designator specifying an intelligent device capable of peer-to-peer communication. Examples are the IBM PC, PC XT, PC AT, and Personal System/2.

**PU 4.** An IBM Corp. Systems Network Architecture (SNA) designator specifying a communications controller such as a 37x5 with Network Control Program (NCP).

**PU 5.** An IBM Corp. Systems Network Architecture (SNA) designator specifying an IBM host processor of the 370 family, such as a 43xx, 303x, 308x, or 309x, with Virtual Telecommunications Access Method (VTAM) and having System Services Control Point (SSCP) capabilities.

**public data network (PDN).** An international term referring to public data networks operated in packet-switched mode.

**public service commission.** An agency charged with regulating public services, including but not restricted to telecommunications service, in the public interest and for the public good. Such commissions usually are organized on a state-by-state basis. May also be referred to as public utility commission.

**public switched digital service (PSDS).** 1. A service offered by the Bell Operating Companies. 2. AT&T's Accunet service.

**public switched telephone network (PSTN).** The publicly available dial-up telephone network.

**public utility commission (PUC).** *See* public service commission.

**PUC.** Public utility commission. *See also* public service commission.

**pulse.** An abrupt, short-duration change in energy from one state to another and back. Pulses normally are used to convey information.

**pulse amplitude modulation (PAM).** Amplitude modulation of a carrier using pulses of varying energy levels (amplitude) to transmit information from the source to the destination.

**pulse code modulation (PCM).** A method of assigning a digital value to samples of a voice signal. The device that performs the digital conversion is called a codec.

**pulse duration modulation (PDM).** A method of carrying digital information by varying the duration of fixed-frequency pulses.

**pulse modulation.** A general method of carrying digital information on any system that uses fixed-frequency pulses to transmit information from the source to the destination. Examples are pulse amplitude modulation and pulse duration modulation.

**pulse position modulation (PPM).** A method of carrying digital information by varying the position in time, as measured from a defined reference point, of fixed-frequency pulses. The time duration of the pulses is not varied.

**pulse width modulation (PWM).** The method of carrying digital information on variable-width pulses of a single analog frequency. May also be referred to as pulse duration modulation.

**PVC.** *See* permanent virtual circuit.

**PWM.** *See* pulse width modulation.

# Q

**Q.921.** In Integrated Services Digital Network (ISDN) technology, a CCITT/ISO data link layer protocol used in the D channel.

**Q.931.** In Integrated Services Digital Network (ISDN) technology, a CCITT/ISO network layer protocol used in the D channel.

**QAM.** *See* quadrature amplitude modulation.

**Q-bit.** The qualifier bit in an X.25 packet that the data terminal equipment uses to indicate that it wants to transmit data at more than one level.

**Q-bus.** The internal interconnection structure of the VAX family of Digital Equipment Corp. computers.

**QLLC.** *See* Qualified Logical Link Control.

**QOS.** *See* quality of service.

**QSAM.** *See* quadrature sideband amplitude modulation.

**QTAM.** *See* Queued Telecommunications Access Method.

**quad.** A slang term for a cable conductor with two twisted-pair wires or four single, untwisted wires that are separately insulated.

**quadrature amplitude modulation (QAM).** A method of combining amplitude modulation with phase shift modulation that allows for the transfer of several bits of information at the same time, expressed as one of 16 or 32 different states.

**quadrature sideband amplitude modulation (QSAM).** A form of quadrature amplitude modulation using sideband frequency transmission.

**Qualified Logical Link Control (QLLC).** An IBM Corp. data link control protocol that allows Systems Network Architecture systems to operate over CCITT X.25 packet-switched networks.

**quality of service (QOS).** A parameter used to describe the attributes of a variety of network functions, such as delays and access probability.

**quantization.** The process by which the continuous range of values of an input signal is divided into subranges and a discrete value of the output is assigned to each value of the subrange.

**quantization error.** An error introduced by the quantization process. For example, an error will be introduced if a continuous analog signal is represented in digital form, and the error will be equal to one half of the least-significant digit.

## queuing

**queue.** An ordered accumulation of data or transactions stored for later processing.

**Queued Telecommunications Access Method (QTAM).** An IBM Corp. communications control protocol that implements a service queue to eliminate the need to block access when the service unit is busy.

**queuing.** The process whereby communications calls, processing requests, processes, and so forth are stacked or held so that they can be worked with in sequences.

# R

**RACE.** *See* Research and Development for Advanced Communications.

**radial wiring.** A wiring scheme in which all wires run from a single point to their destination by the shortest route.

**radio frequency (RF).** Any coherent electromagnetic radiation. The minimum frequency of such radiation is approximately 15 kilohertz.

**radio frequency interference (RFI).** Transmission interference (noise) at frequencies above 15 kilohertz.

**RAM.** *See* random access memory.

**random access memory (RAM).** Memory that can be dynamically written to or read. Memory that the user can access at any point with relative ease and without reading all previous records.

**random retry.** The process whereby a device on an Ethernet (Carrier Sense Multiple Access with Collision Detection) network that has failed to gain access to the network waits a random period of time before it tries again.

**rate center.** A specific geographic point used by telephone companies when determining distances for rate-setting purposes.

**rate of information transfer (RIT).** The amount of information transferred per unit time from one part of a system to another part of the same system.

**RBOC.** *See* Regional Bell Operating Company.

**reachable node.** Any node in a packet-switched network to which a specific node can direct packets.

**read-only memory (ROM).** Nonvolatile memory that can be read but not changed.

**real-time processing.** Processing that takes place at the same real-world time that a transaction occurs. Real-time systems may also be referred to as event-driven systems.

**reassembly.** The process whereby segments of a message received at the transport layer of an Open Systems Interconnect (OSI)-based architecture are placed into a session layer buffer as a single sequential message stream.

**receive-only (RO) device.** 1. A teleprinter that can receive but not transmit signals. 2. Any device that can receive but not transmit signals. A standard computer printer is a good example.

**relative transmission level**

**receiver clock.** The electronic part of a receiving interface that determines where one bit ends and the next begins. In synchronous transmission, the receiver clock may have to be synchronized with the transmitter's clock.

**reception congestion.** The condition under which an input point or port at a switching point in a network cannot accept any incoming data.

**redirector.** A set of higher-level software services in a layered architecture that route requests from user programs to resources such as files, printers, and programs throughout a network.

**redundant bits.** In connection with a transmission control protocol, all control bits that can be removed without a loss of transmitted information.

**redundant circuits.** Transmission paths available for use if the primary circuit fails or is otherwise unavailable.

**reference edge.** The position in a data-carrying signal used as a reference point for all specification measurements. May also be referred to as the guide edge.

**reference noise.** A specific level of transmission circuit noise with which all other noise levels can be compared.

**regenerator.** A digital repeater that receives signals and regenerates them before retransmission. All effects of external noise and transmission distortion can be removed with this process. Regenerators are often referred to as repeaters.

**Regional Bell Operating Company (RBOC).** One of the seven regional holding companies in the U.S. created by the breakup of AT&T. RBOCs are responsible for all local telephone services and operate in a variety of other communications markets.

**regional center.** The Class 1 telephone company switching center used to connect geographic sections of the country.

**register.** A temporary electronic data storage device used to hold data before it is processed.

**relative transmission level.** A measure of transmission medium quality established by comparing the power level of a fixed-frequency transmission at a specific point with the power level of the same frequency at a reference point. The reference point is normally the source transmission interface.

**relay.** 1. A device that receives transmission from one communications channel and retransmits it to another, thereby extending the transmission distance. 2. An electrically operated switch.

**remote job entry (RJE).** A computer operation that allows a processing job to be submitted from a remote point and the results to be delivered back to that point.

**Remote Job Entry (RJE) protocols.** A set of upper-level protocols used in IBM Corp. communications processing for the remote submission and execution of jobs.

**remote log on.** The process of logging on to a computer from a remote point in a network.

**remote node.** As "seen" by a specific node, a remote node is any other node within the same network.

**Remote Procedure Call (RPC).** The process used in Transmission Control Protocol/Internet Protocol (TCP/IP) UNIX environments to implement a specific process on a local or remote network node.

**remote resource access software.** Software facilities that allow one computer to access resources attached to another computer. Remote resource access is normally implemented as a set of higher-level services in a layered network architecture.

**remote station.** A device attached to its controlling point by a transmission link.

**Remote Telecommunications Access Method (RTAM).** An access method used by peripheral devices to access program resources in a non-IBM Corp. Systems Network Architecture (SNA) system.

**Renpac.** A CCITT X.25 packet-switched network operated in Brazil by the Brazilian government.

**repeater.** A device that receives a signal, performs some function such as amplification or regeneration, then retransmits the signal. In a data sense, a repeater is considered a bit store-and-forward device.

**reperforator.** A device that automatically punches paper tape from received signals.

**Request for Comment (RFC).** The procedure used by the Internet community to exchange ideas and establish standards and specifications. Overseeing control is exercised within the U.S. Department of Defense by the SRI International Network Information Center. *Address:* 333

Ravenswood Rd., Rm. EJ291, Menlo Park, CA 94025. Information on RFCs is available online to users who can access the SRI-ARPANET host.

**request to send (RTS).** A physical layer signal sent from transmitting equipment to a modem requesting clearance to send data.

**Research and Development for Advanced Communications (RACE).** A European community endeavor aimed at creating advanced communications networks.

**reservation access.** A method whereby a device accesses a network on a reservation basis. A controlling node normally handles access reservation requests and determines access.

**residual error rate.** As defined by the International Standards Organization (ISO), the remaining error rate after all protocol-specified attempts at correction have been made.

**response time.** 1. In a general sense, the time required for a system to provide a response to an external stimulus. 2. In computer systems, the time required for a computer to provide output after receiving input. 3. In network applications, response time may refer to the time required for a network to respond to a request for service.

**retransmissions on error.** An error correction method whereby data is retransmitted when an error is detected.

**retransmissive star.** A device used in fiber-optic transmission systems that receives a signal from one incoming fiber and retransmits it to many outgoing fibers.

**retry.** In IBM Corp.'s Binary Synchronous Communications (Bisync) protocol, the process of retransmitting a block of data a predefined number of times in an attempt to produce error-free data transfer.

**return bandpass.** The frequency range in a broadband transmission system used to receive signals.

**reverse channel.** A facility in certain modems that allows for reception of low-speed control information on the transmit line of a half-duplex service. The low-speed signals are received while the high-speed signals are being transmitted, allowing for a level of full-duplex operation on a half-duplex line.

**reverse interrupt character (RVI).** A control sequence signal that a receiver sends to a transmitter while receiving transmitted data, requesting that transmission be stopped so that the receiver can transmit a higher-priority message.

**reversible-form document**

**reversible-form document.** An electronically transferrable document with a fully modifiable form, format, and content.

**RF.** *See* radio frequency.

**RFC.** *See* Request for Comment.

**RFC 902.** The Internet Request for Comment that explains how protocol standards are adopted.

**RFC 920.** The Internet Request for Comment that defines the requirements for establishing a domain. In this context, a domain is the group of computers under the specific control of an establishment registered with the SRI International Network Information Center.

**RFC 963.** The Internet Request for Comment that details the problems with a specific U.S. Department of Defense standard for internetworking and proposes solutions.

**RFC 1000.** The Internet Request for Comment (RFC) that catalogs and cross references other RFCs.

**RFC 1131.** An Internet protocol for controlling internetwork routing functions.

**RFC 1195.** An Internet protocol for controlling routing layer-to-routing layer transfers of both Internet Protocol (IP) and Open Systems Interconnect (OSI) packets.

**RFI.** *See* radio frequency interference.

**ring indicator.** A modem interface signal defined by RS 232-C that indicates to the attached terminal that an incoming call is present.

**ring polling.** The process whereby devices are polled sequentially to determine if they have data to transmit. When the last device has been polled and any data transmitted, the polling begins again with the first device in the sequence.

**ring topology.** The network structure whereby devices are connected in a physical ring. IBM Corp. uses this structure in its token-passing local area network implementation.

**RIT.** *See* rate of information transfer.

**RJE.** *See* remote job entry.

**RO.** *See* receive-only device.

**ROM.** *See* read-only memory.

**round trip delay.** The time it takes for an electrical signal to travel from one end of a medium to the other and back.

**route.** The path through a network used to transfer transmission frames, packets, or data units from source to destination.

**route indicator.** An address code in a transmission frame or packet header that specifies the final destination address for the information. This will remain constant even if intermediate point-to-point addresses change during the transmission process.

**router.** A device that performs routing functions — possibly altering physical, data link, and network layer protocols — within a network or between dissimilar networks.

**route table.** A database used by the network layer in a layered architecture to store information against which routing decisions will be made.

**route through.** The process whereby intermediate nodes transfer messages from source to destination. This process is normally referred to as packet switching.

**routing algorithm.** The rules by which routing decisions are made at the network layer. Examples are least-cost routing and least-hops routing.

**Routing Information Protocol (RIP).** A TCP/IP Internet protocol used to control the exchange of information between hosts and gateways.

**routing layer.** The layer in a structured layered network architecture responsible for creating the physical path between the source and destination.

**routing node.** A network node charged with making routing decisions.

**RPC.** *See* Remote Procedure Call.

**R reference point.** In Integrated Services Digital Network (ISDN) technology, the point at which non-ISDN terminals are connected to an ISDN interface via a terminal adapter.

**RTAM.** *See* Remote Telecommunications Access Method.

**RTS.** *See* request to send.

**RVI.** *See* reverse interrupt character.

**RZ (return to zero) encoding.** A physical level transmission encoding scheme where a positive or negative pulse is used to define binary bits and the signal is always returned to zero during a specified time cell. RZ encoding is used heavily in synchronous transmissions.

# S

**SAA.** *See* Systems Application Architecture.

**SAFENET.** *See* Survivable Adaptable Fiber Network.

**SAN.** *See* small area network.

**S and T reference point.** In Integrated Services Digital Network (ISDN) technology, the connection point for ISDN-type terminals.

**SAP.** *See* service access point.

**SASE.** *See* Special Application Service Element.

**satellite.** A receiving and transmitting device orbiting the earth and used to relay signals over great distances.

**satellite relay.** An active or passive satellite repeater that transfers signals from one earth station to another.

**scattering.** The diffusion of a light beam within an optical fiber medium caused by minor variations in the material. The result is signal loss.

**scramble.** To randomize the sequence of transmitted data, thereby providing a level of security.

**SCS.** *See* SNA character string.

**SDH.** *See* Synchronous Digital Hierarchy.

**SDLC.** *See* Synchronous Data Link Control.

**SDM.** *See* subrate data multiplexer.

**SDN.** *See* Software Defined Network.

**SDU.** *See* service data unit.

**seamless connection.** A connection that is completely transparent to the user.

**secondary station.** A node that receives data from a designated primary station.

**segment.** In a bus-based local area network, a single piece of the transmission medium. Segments are normally connected together with repeaters.

**segmentation.** The process whereby the transport layer in a layered architecture breaks down the sequential data stream from the session layer buffer into numbered messages or logical data units for transmission through a network.

## session layer

**selection.** In IBM Corp. terminology, the process whereby a computer contacts an external device in preparation for a message transfer.

**sequencing.** The process of dividing long messages into shorter blocks or packets and appending an identifying number to each.

**Sequential Packet Exchange (SPX).** A transport layer protocol developed by Novell Inc. and used in NetWare implementations.

**serial interface.** The electronic interface between a transmitting or receiving device and a single transmission channel.

**Serial Line Internet Protocol (SLIP).** A packet framing protocol that controls the process of transferring Transmission Control Protocol/ Internet Protocol (TCP/IP) packets across a serial line.

**serial transmission.** The process whereby binary bits are transmitted one at a time. Serial transmission is used heavily in data communications applications. Compare with parallel transmission, normally used only between a computer and local high-speed peripherals.

**server.** A hardware device or software routine that provides one or more predefined services to a population of using entities, such as nodes on a network.

**service access point (SAP).** In connection with a service provider, the point at which a request for service or a notification of provision is made. The equivalent term in a UNIX environment is *socket*.

**service data unit (SDU).** A defined unit of data (message) passed from one client of a service for transmission to another client.

**service provider.** A software module that provides services to other software modules. The term is used when describing functions in the software layers of a layered network architecture.

**service requester.** The software module in a layered software environment that requests a service. Also referred to as the client.

**serving area.** The area around a broadcast transmission station where the signal strength is above a defined minimum.

**session.** The functional connection between two devices that allows them to communicate.

**session layer.** The name of the layer within the Open Systems Interconnect (OSI) architecture responsible for creating and maintaining a transfer session and for such system services as user-to-system address transformation, access control, and security. May also be referred to as the session level.

**S/F.** *See* store and forward.

**Shannon limit.** A measure of the quality of the information in a message. The Shannon limit of a voice-grade line is approximately 2,400 signal state changes per second.

**shared server.** A device that provides predefined services to multiple network nodes in more than one network area or domain.

**SHF.** *See* super high frequency.

**shielded twisted pair.** Twisted-pair wire with additional electrical shielding wrapped around the insulated conductors, normally in the form of aluminum foil.

**shielding.** The material surrounding a transmission medium to reduce or eliminate the effects of radiated electromagnetic transmission from, or reception by, the medium.

**short circuit.** The condition wherein conductors that are supposed to be insulated from one another come into direct electrical contact. This is normally considered a fault condition.

**short-haul modem.** A modem designed for use with cable-based systems with distances of up to ten miles. Short-haul modems are used primarily to eliminate the restrictions of the relatively short distances allowed by such specifications as EIA RS 232-C.

**signal conditioning.** The modification of a signal, by amplification or transformation, to make it more suitable for transmission across a specific medium.

**signal converter.** A device that receives signals in one form and transmits them in a different form. Signals may change frequency, form (analog to digital), and so forth.

**signal element.** The smallest unit of a signaling code.

**signal reflection.** If a signal encounters a sudden change in electrical impedance as it is transmitted through a medium, a portion of the signal will be reflected back the way it came. This is particularly problematic if multiple reflections occur in the same medium.

**signal regeneration.** The process whereby a signal is modified to ensure that it meets its original specification.

**signal-to-noise ratio.** A measure of the quality of a transmission defined as the ratio produced by dividing the transmitted signal strength by the strength of the induced noise.

**signal transformation.** The action of modifying one or more characteristics of a signal, such as its maximum value, shape, or timing.

**SII.** *See* Systems Integration Interface.

**silo.** A type of first-in, first-out buffer used with multiplexers.

**Simple Mail Transfer Protocol (SMTP).** A protocol used in UNIX environments for electronic mail transfer across a network. SMTP was created within the Internet community using the Request for Comment (RFC) process.

**Simple Network Management Protocol (SNMP).** A set of rules for performing network management functions. SNMP is approved for use with Transmission Control Protocol/Internet Protocol (TCP/IP) in UNIX environments. SNMP was created within the Internet community using the Request for Comment (RFC) process.

**simplex transmission.** Unidirectional transmission.

**single-mode fiber.** A fiber-optic transmission medium designed to carry light waves at a single frequency.

**single-sideband transmission.** Transmission using one sideband of a carrier.

**sink.** 1. The receiving portion of a data communications system. 2. The point at which transmitted signal electrons are finally removed from the medium.

**SITA.** *See* Société Internationale de Télécommunication Aéronautique.

**SKDP.** A CCITT X.25 packet-switched network operated in Indonesia by the Indonesian government.

**skew.** The time lapse between the transmission of any two signals.

**Skynet.** A proposed AT&T digital service using satellite transmission to connect various Accunet services.

**slave station.** A device, normally on a multipoint line, that can transmit only to a specific controlling node upon that node's request.

**slotted ring.** A local area network medium access control method whereby available time slots are routed around a ring and used by transmitting devices based on the network's set of rules.

**small area network (SAN).** A network generally limited to 100 meters. SANs use specialized communications techniques and are used for process control and other specific real-time computer applications.

## SMDR

**SMDR.** *See* station message detail recording.

**SMDS.** *See* Switched Multimegabit Data Service.

**SMTP.** *See* Simple Mail Transfer Protocol.

**SNA.** *See* Systems Network Architecture.

**SNA character string (SCS).** In IBM Corp.'s Systems Network Architecture (SNA) technology, a type of data string in which data characters and control characters are carried within the same transmission frame.

**SNA Distribution Services (SNADS).** A set of IBM Corp. Systems Network Architecture (SNA) services that allows for the delayed delivery of data to its final destination. The delay is caused by the storing of data at intermediate switching points within the network. SNADS is used in distributed processing and office automation environments.

**SNADS.** *See* SNA Distribution Services.

**SNAP.** *See* Subnetwork Access Protocol.

**SNI.** *See* System Network Interconnection.

**SNMP.** *See* Simple Network Management Protocol.

**SNMP Management Information Base (SNMP-MIB).** Entity definitions for use with the Transmission Control Protocol/Internet Protocol (TCP/IP) and UNIX Simple Network Management Protocol (SNMP).

**SNMP MIB.** *See* SNMP Management Information Base.

**Société Internationale de Télécommunication Aéronautique (SITA).** An organization that operates an international message and data network for the major airlines.

**Society for Worldwide Interbank Financial Telecommunications (SWIFT).** The organization that designed and operates a network to support the information transfer needs of banks and financial institutions.

**Software Defined Network (SDN).** An AT&T service network operating at data rates of up to 56 Kbps.

**SOH.** *See* start of header.

**SOM.** *See* start of message.

**SONET.** *See* Synchronous Optical Network.

**source.** 1. A transmission's starting point. 2. The first transmitting device in a logical data transfer path.

**source service access point (SSAP).** The service access point from which data originated. This information may be carried in the data field of an IEEE 802.3 transmission frame.

**space.** 1. A signal transmitted to signify a logical zero. 2. A keyboard character used to separate words, sequences, and so forth.

**space-division multiplexing.** A method whereby several entities use a single service facility. Within the facility a certain amount of physical space is dedicated to each device. An example is the sharing of a single conduit between floors of a building by providing individual, wire-based physical circuits for each user.

**Special Application Service Element (SASE).** In connection with the International Standards Organization (ISO) Open Systems Interconnect (OSI) layered network architecture, SASE refers to a range of special services provided by the application layer. Such services are normally user defined and include conversational formats and operation dialogs.

**spine network.** A interconnecting network that users access through another network. May also be referred to as a backbone network.

**spiral redundancy check (SRC).** A composite number transmitted with data and used for error checking at the receiver.

**split-stream modem.** A device that combines the functions of a time-division multiplexer and a modem.

**splitter.** A device that separates a single transmission medium into two or more identical channels.

**spot beam.** A narrow-beam satellite transmission method.

**spread spectrum.** A modulation technique in which the information content is spread over a wider bandwidth than the frequency range of the original signal.

**SPX.** *See* Sequential Packet Exchange.

**SRC.** *See* spiral redundancy check.

**SSAP.** *See* source service access point.

**SSCP.** *See* System Services Control Point.

**StarLAN.** A type of local area network designed by AT&T that uses twisted-pair wire and has a transmission speed of 1 Mbps, 5 Mbps, or 10 Mbps.

## start bit

**start bit.** In asynchronous transmission, a bit transmitted to signify that what follows is data. As specified by RS 232-C, the bit is always a logical zero state; therefore, the idle state must be a permanent one. This set of rules helps determine the difference between an idle channel and a damaged channel.

**start of header (SOH).** A transmission control character used to signify the start of a transmission frame header.

**start of message (SOM).** A transmission framing character used in IBM Corp.'s Binary Synchronous Communications (BSC) protocol to signify the start of a specific message.

**start of text (STX).** A transmission framing character used in IBM Corp.'s Binary Synchronous Communications (BSC) protocol to signify the start of a text block within a message transmission sequence.

**star topology.** A network structure where all devices are connected through a single switching point. The voice telephone private branch exchange is an example of such a switching point.

**start/stop transmission.** The asynchronous transmission method that requires each character to be preceded by a start bit and followed by one or more stop bits.

**station.** One of the input, switching, or output points on a communications system. May also be called a node.

**station address.** The unique identifier associated with a specific station.

**station message detail recording (SMDR).** The process whereby details of telephone handset use are centrally recorded. SMDR is used for cost accounting and security and is often implemented as one of the functions of a private branch exchange.

**station terminal equipment (STE).** A CCITT term for a gateway node between international packet-switched networks.

**statistical time-division multiplexing.** The process whereby several slow devices, such as computers and terminals, share a high-speed device such as a transmission line by using time periods based on previously determined statistical-usage requirement patterns. This form of asynchronous time-division multiplexing results in maximum use of the high-speed service.

**stat mux.** An abbreviation for statistical time-division multiplexer.

**STD.** *See* subscriber trunk dialing.

## substitute character (SUB)

**STDM.** *See* synchronous time-division multiplexing.

**STE.** *See* station terminal equipment.

**step index optical fiber.** A fiber that has a constant refractive index at its core but a different refractive index as the outer cladding is approached. This design minimizes losses at the core-cladding interface and is preferred for single-mode, long-distance transmission.

**STM.** *See* synchronous transmission mode.

**stop bit.** In asynchronous transmission, a bit or series of bits used to signify the end of a character. RS 232-C defines this state as the logical one for a specific period of time.

**store and forward (S/F).** A type of transmission service whereby messages or parts of messages are received at an intermediate point in a network and then retransmitted (with or without a delay) to another point in the network.

**strap.** A permanent, wired connection between two or more points.

**StreetTalk.** A system for naming all resources on a Banyan Systems Inc. VINES network. The VINES server software is implemented by a customized version of UNIX.

**STS-1.** *See* Synchronous Transport Signaling Level 1.

**STS-n.** *See* Synchronous Transport Signaling Level n.

**STX.** *See* start of text.

**SUB.** *See* substitute character.

**Subnetwork Access Protocol (SNAP).** A version of the IEEE local area network logical link control frame similar to the more traditional data link level transmission frame that allows for the use of nonstandard higher-level protocols.

**subrate data multiplexer (SDM).** A type of data transmission multiplexer.

**subscriber trunk dialing (STD).** The European version of direct-distance dialing.

**subsplit.** A method of allocating frequencies in a broadband transmission system. Transmit frequencies are in the range of 5 to 32 megahertz, and receive frequencies are in the range of 54 to 300 megahertz.

**substitute character (SUB).** A transmission control character used in place of a character found to be in error.

## super high frequency (SHF)

**super high frequency (SHF).** Transmission frequencies in the range of 3,000 to 30,000 megahertz.

**Survivable Adaptable Fiber Network (SAFENET).** A U.S. Navy experimental fiber-based local area network designed to survive conventional and limited nuclear battle conditions.

**SVC.** *See* switched virtual circuit.

**SVID.** *See* System V Interface Definition.

**SWIFT.** *See* Society for Worldwide Interbank Financial Telecommunications.

**Switched Multimegabit Data Service (SMDS).** A service planned by the U.S. regional telephone companies based on the IEEE 802.6 metropolitan network specifications.

**switched virtual circuit (SVC).** 1. A virtual connection established between entities at the beginning of a transmission session and maintained throughout the session. 2. A CCITT X.25 term used to describe a packet-switched service similar to dial-up service.

**switching.** The process of transferring a connection from one circuit to another by connecting the two circuits.

**switching center.** A device or collection of devices that routes incoming signals to the proper outgoing lines.

**SYFA Virtual Network.** The network architecture used by Computer Automation.

**SYN.** *See* synchronous control character.

**synchronization bits.** Bits transmitted from source to destination for the purpose of time clock synchronization of the transmitting and receiving devices.

**synchronous control character (SYN).** A transmission control character used in synchronous transmission to provide a signal in the absence of any other character. SYN is defined by IBM Corp.'s Binary Synchronous Communications (BSC) protocol.

**Synchronous Data Link Control (SDLC).** The data link control used for point-to-point transmission control by IBM Corp. in Systems Network Architecture (SNA) environments. SDLC is also used in some non-SNA applications. SDLC is a bit-oriented protocol.

**Synchronous Digital Hierarchy (SDH).** The CCITT equivalent of the U.S. Synchronous Optical Network (SONET) transmission service.

## System Services Control Point (SSCP)

**Synchronous Optical Network (SONET).** An optical transmission network proposed by Bellcore that operates at or above T3 speeds (44.736 Mbps).

**synchronous time-division multiplexing (STDM).** A time-division multiplexing method whereby devices have access to a high-speed transmission medium at fixed time periods independent of likely load.

**synchronous transmission.** The movement of binary bits across a transmission medium where the transmitter and receiver have synchronized clocks. Synchronization is accomplished either by the transmission of special synchronizing bits or by taking timing from the transmitted message. During synchronous transmission, it is normal to place controlling information (framing) around complete messages.

**synchronous transmission mode (STM).** The synchronous transmission capability of a system that is capable of both synchronous and asynchronous transmission. For example, STM is used to denote the synchronous capabilities of Broadband Integrated Services Digital Network (B-ISDN) service.

**Synchronous Transport Signaling Level 1 (STS-1).** The basic signaling rate for a Synchronous Optical Network (SONET) transmission medium. The STS-1 rate is 51.8 Mbps.

**Synchronous Transport Signaling Level n (STS-n).** A definition of the transmission speed of a Synchronous Optical Network (SONET) transmission medium where, currently, $n$ is an integer between 1 and 48 and relates to the multiplier to be applied to the basic STS-1 51.8-Mbps transmission speed. STS-48 is 48 times faster than STS-1, with a resulting speed of 2.5 gigabits per second.

**System V Interface Definition (SVID).** A UNIX application-to-system software interface developed and supported by AT&T. The interface is similar to POSIX.

**System Network Interconnection (SNI).** A service defined by IBM Corp. that allows for the interconnection of separately defined and controlled Systems Network Architecture (SNA) networks.

**System Services Control Point (SSCP).** An IBM Corp. Systems Network Architecture (SNA) term for the software that manages the available connection services to be utilized by the Network Control Program (NCP). There is only one SSCP in an SNA network domain, and the software normally resides in the host processor, which is a member of the IBM System/370 mainframe family.

## Systems Application Architecture (SAA)

**Systems Application Architecture (SAA).** An IBM Corp. architecture aimed at creating fully integrated systems at the application level.

**Systems Integration Interface (SII).** As used in the definition of the proposed multivendor integration architecture sponsored by Nippon Telegraph and Telephone (NTT) of Japan, SII specifies any set of standardized services used to connect computer-based systems.

**Systems Network Architecture (SNA).** IBM Corp.'s traditional approach to networking that uses a Network Control Program (NCP) to create circuit-switched connections between physical units that implement processes under the control of groups of higher-level protocols called logical units.

# T

**T1 carrier.** A specialized digital transmission system developed by AT&T that operates at a total speed of 1.544 Mbps using time-division multiplexing techniques. A T1 carrier can support 24 voice circuits.

**T2 carrier.** A specialized digital transmission system developed by AT&T that operates at a total speed of 6.312 Mbps using time-division multiplexing techniques. A T2 carrier can support 96 voice circuits.

**T3 carrier.** A specialized digital transmission system developed by AT&T that operates at a total speed of 44.736 Mbps using time-division multiplexing techniques. A T3 carrier can support 672 voice circuits.

**T4 carrier.** A specialized digital transmission system developed by AT&T that operates at 273 Mbps. A T4 carrier can support 4,032 voice circuits.

**TA.** *See* terminal adapter.

**tail circuit.** The connection from a satellite or microwave receiver to a user's equipment location.

**TAM.** *See* telecommunications access method.

**tandem data circuit.** A transmission circuit passing through two or more serially connected data terminating equipment devices.

**tandem exchange.** A telephone switching center that handles traffic between local exchanges.

**tap.** 1. A connector that couples to a cable without blocking the passage of signals along the cable. 2. The process whereby attachment is made to a cable for the express purpose of monitoring the data flowing along the cable.

**TASI.** *See* time assignment speech interpolation.

**task.** A computer program in execution.

**task-to-task communication.** The process whereby one operative computer program exchanges data with another. May also be called program-to-program communication.

**TAT-8.** The eighth transatlantic telephone cable and the first to use fiber-optic transmission media.

**TC.** *See* transmission control characters.

**TCAM.** *See* Telecommunications Access Method.

# T-carrier

**T-carrier.** A series of digital transmission services, at speeds of 1.544 Mbps or higher, established by AT&T. The T notation signifies time-division multiplexing.

**TCM.** *See* time-compression multiplexer.

**T-connector.** A coaxial cable connector, named after its shape, that allows devices to be attached to a single multidrop conductor.

**TCP/IP.** *See* Transmission Control Protocol/Internet Protocol.

**TCU.** *See* terminal control unit.

**TDM.** *See* time-division multiplexer.

**TDMA.** *See* time-division multiple access.

**TDX.** *See* time-division multiplexer.

**TE1.** *See* Terminal Equipment Type 1.

**TE2.** *See* Terminal Equipment Type 2.

**Technical Office Protocol (TOP).** A seven-layer network architecture designed for office automation that uses International Standards Organization (ISO) or CCITT specifications at each level. TOP was defined by Boeing Vertol Corp. and is now controlled by the MAP/TOP (Manufacturing Automation Protocol/Technical Office Protocol) Users Group.

**telco.** A popular abbreviation for telephone company.

**telecommunications.** A general term for voice or data communications implemented using coded signals over a transmission medium.

**telecommunications access method (TAM).** Software used to enable remote devices to transfer data to, and receive data from, host processors.

**Telecommunications Access Method (TCAM).** One of the telecommunications access methods used by non-Systems Network Architecture (SNA) IBM Corp. systems to control the connection of secondary, remote devices to a host processor and manage the data transfer.

**Telecommunications Industry Association (TIA).** An organization concerned with standards conformance and product testing in the telecommunications industry.

**telecommuting.** The process whereby an employee works at home on a computer or terminal connected via a communications channel to a host at the employer's office.

## Telrate International Quotations (TIQ)

**telecopier.** Another name for a facsimile machine.

**telegraphy.** A data communications process wherein current reversals are used to indicate data bits. The maximum transmission rate of such current reversal-based systems is normally less then 100 bps.

**telemedicine.** The provision of health-care services from a distance using networks supporting audio, video, and computer data transmissions.

**telemetry.** Transmission and collection of data obtained by sensing conditions in a real-time environment.

**TELEPAC.** 1. A packet-switched network implemented in Switzerland and operated by the Swiss government. 2. A packet-switched network implemented in Portugal and operated by the Portuguese government.

**telephony.** The electronic transfer of voice communication.

**teleprocessing.** The use of systems that combine data communications, data processing, and human/machine interfacing to allow computational processes to be executed at a location other than the data entry point or information extraction point.

**Teletex.** A high-speed, ASCII-based text transmission service designed to replace Telex.

**teletext.** One-way transmission, normally broadcast, designed for the public distribution of graphics and text.

**teletypewriter exchange (TWX) service.** A teletype-based dial-up network owned by Western Union Corp. TWX service is available in the U.S. and Canada.

**Telex.** A text transmission service offered by Western Union Corp. based on Baudot code and operating at 50 bps.

**TELENET.** A private, commercially available network providing both packet-switched and circuit-switched service to subscribers in North America, Europe and some parts of Asia.

**TELNET Remote Login Protocol.** A virtual terminal service specified by the U.S. Department of Defense and implemented by most versions of UNIX.

**Telrate International Quotations (TIQ).** A market data information subscription service operated by Telrate International Co. over a network that uses proprietary protocols to enhance security and other functions.

## temporary text delay (TTD)

**temporary text delay (TTD).** A transmission control character used in IBM Corp.'s Binary Synchronous Communications (BSC) protocol to signify a delay in the transmission of text components within an overall message.

**terminal.** A device at the beginning or end of a transmission system, normally a nonintelligent keyboard, video display device, or printer.

**terminal adapter (TA).** In Integrated Services Digital Network (ISDN) technology, an interface that links terminals that are not compatible with ISDN to an ISDN service.

**terminal control unit (TCU).** A device used to control a local group of terminals. May also be called a terminal server or cluster controller.

**terminal emulation.** The process whereby a computer or terminal is made to look and perform like a specific type of terminal. Terminal emulation (using hardware, software or both) is the most common method of accessing a minicomputer or mainframe from a PC.

**Terminal Equipment Type 1 (TE1).** In Integrated Services Digital Network (ISDN) technology, a type of terminal compatible with ISDN.

**Terminal Equipment Type 2 (TE2).** In Integrated Services Digital Network (ISDN) technology, a type of terminal that must be connected to ISDN via a specially designated point, normally an RS 232 or RS 449 interface.

**terminal interface processor (TIP).** A computational device used to interface equipment to ARPANET, TELNET, or another defined network.

**terminal node.** In IBM Corp.'s Systems Network Architecture (SNA), a network device that cannot be programmed by the user.

**terminal server.** A computer used to connect sets of terminals to a network that requires the implementation of control processes too complex for individual terminals to perform.

**terminated line.** A communications line terminated by a resistance equal to the line impedance to eliminate reflections.

**terminator.** A device used to provide a specified electrical environment, such as resistance to ground. Terminators typically are used at the ends of a cable.

**terrestrial facilities.** Long-distance, nonsatellite transmission facilities.

**test center.** A facility designed to provide access to all network components for testing purposes.

**text.** The part of a transmitted message that carries the information.

**TFTP.** *See* Trivial File Transfer Protocol.

**ThickWire.** Standard 50-ohm, Ethernet IEEE 802.3 coaxial cable.

**ThinWire.** The 75-ohm coaxial cable listed in IEEE 802.3 specifications and used in some Ethernet installations.

**TIA.** *See* Telecommunications Industry Association.

**Ticker III and Ticker IV.** The stock market data distribution system operated by Standard and Poors Co. Access is limited principally to trading members of the U.S. Stock Exchange.

**tie line.** A dedicated or private line a telephone company supplies to a subscriber. A tie line is not part of the public switched network.

**time assignment speech interpolation (TASI).** A voice telephone mechanism whereby the actual presence of a speech signal activates circuit use. The result is more efficient use of the transmission facility.

**time-compression multiplexer (TCM).** A form of multiplexer using time compression rather than time division to allow high-speed transmission over a local-loop facility.

**time-division multiple access (TDMA).** A satellite communications method whereby multiple earth stations have time-slot access to the full transponder bandwidth for short periods.

**time-division multiplexer (TDM or TDX).** A device that enables more than one low-speed device to share a high-speed line by allowing each device a time period on the line.

**time-out.** A control function whereby a process is discontinued if an expected event does not occur within a predefined period of time.

**time sharing.** The sharing of a resource between two or more users on a predefined or calculated time basis.

**time to live.** A controlling field used in Transmission Control Protocol/Internet Protocol (TCP/IP) transmissions to limit the amount of time a package can exist in a network, thereby eliminating package looping.

**timing slip.** A sudden timing delay change during high-speed digital transmission often caused by the use of T1 carriers from different suppliers.

**TIP.** *See* terminal interface processor.

**TIQ.** *See* Telrate International Quotations.

**token**

**token.** A short transmission frame used in a tokens-bus or token-ring network to control network access. The frame normally consists of a set of bits defining the start of the frame, a set of controlling bits, and a set of bits defining the end of the frame.

**token bus.** A local area network configuration in which a physical bus structure is made to perform like a logical ring and access is controlled by a rotating token.

**token holding time.** The time during which a device in a token-passing system may transmit after it has received the access-control token.

**token ring.** A local area network configuration that uses a physical ring structure and in which network device access is controlled by a rotating token.

**token-tree LAN.** A type of local area network with a topology in the form of branches interconnected via active hubs. Using a token-passing scheme, the active hubs grant nodes access to the medium.

**toll center.** Any Class 4 telephone company central office facility where time- and distance-based toll charge information is calculated and recorded. Also referred to as toll office.

**TOP.** *See* Technical Office Protocol.

**top-level domain.** A certain segment of a network in the Transmission Control Protocol/Internet Protocol (TCP/IP) UNIX environment. A network is segmented into a hierarchy of domains or groupings. In the U.S.-based Internet network, there are six top-level domains: com (commercial organizations), edu (educational organizations), gov (government agencies), mil (Milnet hosts), net (networking organizations), and org (nonprofit organizations). The next lower level relates to specific companies, and the level below to devices within a company.

**topology.** The physical arrangement of devices in a network, regardless of their logical relationships. Types of topologies include star, ring, and bus.

**TOPS.** The operating system used by Digital Equipment Corp.'s DECSYSTEM-10 and DECSYSTEM-20 computers. These computers have been discontinued, but many are still in use.

**Touch Tone.** AT&T's registered trademark for push-button dialing. Each button produces a signal in the form of multiple frequencies or tones.

## transmission

**TP1, TP2, TP3, TP4, TP5.** The various service levels of the ISO IS 8073 Transport Protocol. TP4 is the most popular service level for information system networks and is specified in the U.S. government GOSIP architecture.

**TP4.** *See* Transport Protocol Class Four.

**TPDU.** *See* transport protocol data unit.

**trace block.** *See* trailer.

**traffic flow analysis.** The analysis of data flow within a network before designing and installing communications lines.

**traffic management.** The process of managing the flow of data within a network.

**trailer.** A block of controlling information transmitted at the end of a message to trace error impacts and missing blocks. Also referred to as a trace block.

**transceiver.** 1.In IEEE 802.3 networks, the attachment hardware connecting the controller interface to the transmission cable. The transceiver contains the carrier-sense logic, the transmit/receive logic, and the collision-detect logic. 2. Any device that transmits and receives.

**transducer.** A device that converts a signal's physical properties from one energy form to another. An example is the interface between a computer, which produces electron-based signals, and a fiber-optic transmission medium, which handles photon-based signals.

**transients.** Short-duration transmission signal interruptions.

**transit exchange.** The European equivalent of a tandem exchange.

**transit timing.** A method of eliminating looping between nodes used in the network layer of some packet-switched systems. This method is used in the Internet Protocol (IP) portion of Transmission Control Protocol/Internet Protocol (TCP/IP).

**translator.** 1. A telephone company facility that translates dial pulses or tones into call-processing information. 2. A communications device that receives signals in one form, normally in analog form at a specific frequency, and retransmits them in a different form.

**transmission.** The transfer of information from one point to another using one of many physical methods and one of many media.

# Transmission Control Protocol/Internet Protocol (TCP/IP)

**Transmission Control Protocol/Internet Protocol (TCP/IP).** A transport and network layer set of protocols. TCP/IP was initially implemented in hardware attachment devices used to connect computers to ARPANET. TCP/IP is included in the University of California at Berkeley's UNIX Release 4.2 and in UNIX offerings from many vendors.

**transmission control (TC) characters.** A group of characters used to facilitate or control data transmission. Examples are NAK (not acknowledge) and EOT (end of transmission).

**transmission medium.** Any material used to carry a representation of information such as an electrical or optical representation.

**TRANSPAC.** A packet-switched network implemented in France and operated by the French government.

**transparent mode.** 1. A mode of communication in which the recognition of the control characters is eliminated. 2. A method of operating a communications channel, normally a digital channel, by which the user has full use of the total available bandwidth.

**transponder.** A device that receives a signal, amplifies it, and retransmits it at a different frequency.

**transport layer.** The layer in the Open Systems Interconnect (OSI) network architecture responsible for the end-to-end integrity of transmission throughout a network. This layer is also concerned with flow control and speed matching. Examples of protocols operating at the transport layer include Transmission Control Protocol (TCP) and Digital Equipment Corp.'s Network Services Protocol (NSP).

**Transport Protocol Class Four (TP4).** An International Standards Organization (ISO) transport layer protocol designated as ISO IS 8073 Class Four Service. TP4 was recently adopted by the U.S. Department of Defense and specified in the U.S. Government OSI Profile (GOSIP).

**transport protocol data unit (TPDU).** The form into which the transport layer in a network architecture will format data for use and recognition.

**transverse parity check.** A type of parity checking.

**tree.** A network topology wherein only one route exists between any two nodes.

**Trellis coding.** An error-checking method used in some high-speed modems whereby information on phase and amplitude is added to individual signal elements.

**tribit transmission.** A transmission technique used by some modems in which the states of three bits are transmitted simultaneously.

**tributary station.** A device on a multipoint line that is not the controlling station. May also be called a slave station.

**Trivial File Transfer Protocol (TFTP).** A UNIX-based file transfer protocol. TFTP is a simplification of the earlier Simple File Transfer Protocol (SFTP).

**truncated binary exponential back off.** Another name for exponential back off used in IEEE 802.3 local area networks. In an exponential back-off process, the time delay between successive attempts to transmit a specific frame is increased exponentially.

**trunk.** A single connection line between two switching or routing devices.

**trunk group.** Multiple connections between the same switching centers.

**T-span.** A telephone term for a transmission medium through which a T-carrier system is operated.

**T-tap.** A passive connection used to extract signal data from a transmission line for testing or for other purposes, such as statistical sampling and control.

**TTD.** *See* temporary text delay.

**TTY.** 1. An abbreviation for teletypewriter. 2. The data link control protocol used to control transmission between a teletypewriter and its service network. This protocol is also used to control a wide range of simple, low-cost asynchronous transmissions.

**TTY protocol.** A simple, asynchronous data link protocol used to control the transmission of individual characters. Error detection is performed using a simple parity check.

**turnaround time.** In a half-duplex transmission system, the actual time taken for a device to change its status from transmitter to receiver.

**twinaxial cable.** Transmission cable that has two separate conductors at its center and an axial shield.

**twisted-pair wire.** Two insulated wires twisted together and used for transmission. The twisting creates a low level of noise elimination.

**two-way alternate operation.** Transmission in one direction or the other but not in both simultaneously. More often referred to as half-duplex transmission.

## two-way simultaneous operation

**two-way simultaneous operation.** Transmission and reception at the same time. More often referred to as full-duplex transmission.

**TWX.** *See* teletypewriter exchange service.

**TYMNET.** A packet-switched network implemented in the U.S., Europe, and other parts of the world. TYMNET is operated by British Telecom Co. *Address*: British Telecom TYMNET, 2560 N. First St., San Jose, CA 95131.

# U

**UART.** *See* universal asynchronous receiver-transmitter.

**UDP.** *See* User Datagram Protocol.

**uhf.** *See* ultrahigh frequency.

**UI frame.** *See* unnumbered information frame.

**ULANA.** An ongoing U.S. Air Force project aimed at creating a series of interconnected local area networks using Transmission Control Protocol/Internet Protocol (TCP/IP) as the unifying transport layer.

**ultrahigh frequency (uhf).** Transmission frequencies in the range of 300 to 3,000 megahertz.

**ULTRIX.** A version of the UNIX operating system developed and supported by Digital Equipment Corp. ULTRIX conforms to current standards and runs on VAX computers as well as certain Digital workstations.

**unbalanced to ground.** A characteristic of specific two-wire systems and systems with more than two wires whereby the impedance to ground is different for each conductor.

**uncontrolled terminal.** A user terminal that is online at all times and that does not contain the logic that would allow it to be polled, called, or otherwise controlled by the device to which it is connected.

**UNIBUS.** The internal structure of the PDP-11 family of Digital Equipment Corp. computers.

**unidirectional bus.** A distribution conductor or set of conductors that can transfer data in one direction only.

**Unified Network Management Architecture (UNMA).** A network management architecture defined by AT&T for use in UNIX environments. UNMA adheres to the International Standards Organization (ISO) Open Systems Interconnect (OSI) model.

**UNINET.** A packet-switched network implemented in the U.S.

**uninterruptable power supply (UPS).** A power supply used as a backup in the event of a power line failure. A UPS may consist of batteries, a generator, or both.

**United States Independent Telephone Association (USITA).** An organization supporting the needs of independent telephone companies.

## universal asynchronous receiver-transmitter (UART)

**universal asynchronous receiver-transmitter (UART).** A device that performs the parallel-to-serial translations on data to be used for asynchronous transmission and the serial-to-parallel translation of asynchronous data received by a computer. This process typically is carried out using a single integrated circuit chip and is required to match the internal parallel structure of a computer and the serial requirements of most communications lines.

**universal synchronous/asynchronous receiver-transmitter (USART).** A device that performs parallel-to-serial translation of data to be transmitted synchronously or asynchronously. It also translates synchronous or asynchronous received serial data to parallel data. These functions are normally accomplished by a single integrated circuit chip.

**universal synchronous receiver-transmitter (USRT).** A device that performs parallel-to-serial translation of data to be transmitted synchronously and translates received serial data into parallel data. This process is normally carried out by a single integrated circuit chip.

**UNIX.** An operating system developed by AT&T that is popular in part because of its ability to operate on a wide variety of hardware. UNIX was developed to control multiprocessor systems and is therefore ideal for networking environments.

**UNIX-to-UNIX Copy Program (UUCP).** A standard UNIX utility for exchanging information between two UNIX-based machines in a network. UUCP may also be referred to as the UNIX-to-UNIX Communications Protocol and is widely used for electronic mail transfer.

**UNMA.** *See* Unified Network Management Architecture.

**unnumbered information frame (UI frame).** A transmission frame generated by the High-Level Data Link Control (HDLC) data link protocol, where no flow control and error control are implemented.

**unshielded twisted-pair wire.** Twisted-pair wire with no outer shielding. The lack of outer shielding reduces the noise elimination of the conductors, but improves the maximum attainable transmission speed.

**uplink.** A ground-to-satellite transmission link.

**UPS.** *See* uninterruptable power supply.

**uptime.** The amount of time a network or other facility is available for general use.

**U Reference Point.** In the U.S., the point that defines the line of demarcation between user-owned and supplier-owned Integrated Services Digital Network (ISDN) facilities.

**USART.** *See* universal synchronous/asynchronous receiver-transmitter.

**USENET.** A news-gathering network of more than 1,000 host processors situated around the world.

**User Datagram Protocol (UDP).** A packet format included in the Transmission Control Protocol/Internet Protocol (TCP/IP) suite and used for short user messages and control messages. The transmission of UDPs is unacknowledged.

**USITA.** *See* United States Independent Telephone Association.

**USRT.** *See* universal synchronous receiver-transmitter.

**UUCP.** *See* UNIX-to-UNIX Copy Program.

# V

**VACC.** *See* value-added common carrier.

**value-added common carrier (VACC).** A common carrier that provides some network service other than simple end-to-end data transmission. Services include least-cost routing, accounting data, and delivery clarification.

**value-added network (VAN).** A network that provides some value more than basic transmission service. Examples are TELNET and Tymnet.

**VAN.** *See* value-added network.

**variable quantizing level (VQL).** A speech encoding technique that results in a 32-Kbps signal.

**VENUS-P.** A CCITT X.25 packet-switched network operated in Japan by Nippon Telephone and Telegraph (NTT) Co.

**vertical redundancy check (VRC).** A parity check used in conjunction with a longitudinal redundancy check for parallel data transfer.

**very high frequency (VHF).** A transmission frequency in the range of 30 to 300 megahertz.

**very low frequency (VLF).** The portion of the electromagnetic spectrum with frequencies between 3 and 30 kilohertz.

**very small aperture terminal (VSAT).** A satellite-based transmission and reception service that requires small, relatively inexpensive antennas.

**VGPL.** *See* voice-grade private line.

**VHF.** *See* very high frequency.

**video conferencing.** The use of remote conferencing facilities that include video signals.

**video signal.** A signal having the frequency range normally required to carry visual information. The range is 1 to 6 megahertz.

**Videotex.** An ISO/CCITT-endorsed method for transmitting and displaying information in public access database systems.

**Viewdata.** A form of Videotex service offered by British Telecom.

**VINES.** *See* Virtual Networking System.

**virtual circuit.** A connection that performs as if it were a physical connection between the source and the destination. The connection may use different facilities during a transfer session, but the end-to-end characteristics remain constant.

## voice frequency

**virtual FAX.** A device comprising a personal computer and an image scanner that can duplicate the functions of a facsimile machine.

**Virtual Machine Facility (VM/370).** An IBM Corp. System/370 operating system that allows for the concurrent operation of many virtual machines on the same computer.

**Virtual Memory System (VMS).** The operating system used by Digital Equipment Corp. VAX computers.

**Virtual Networking System (VINES).** A hardware-independent local area network operating system developed by Banyan Systems Inc. VINES is based on the UNIX operating system.

**virtual private network (VPN).** A public carrier service that operates as a set of private circuits, with the same characteristics.

**Virtual Telecommunications Access Method (VTAM).** The access method used by IBM Corp. Systems Network Architecture (SNA)-based systems.

**virtual terminal.** A network node made to look and perform like a terminal attached to another network node by implementating presentation layer and session layer software services.

**Virtual Terminal Protocol (VTP).** An International Standards Organization (ISO) standard for virtual terminal service.

**VLF.** *See* very low frequency.

**VM/370.** *See* Virtual Machine Facility.

**VMS.** *See* Virtual Memory System.

**VMS OSI Transport Services (VOTS).** A Digital Equipment Corp. software product that modifies Digital's DECnet transport layer to conform to the International Standards Organization (ISO) Transport Protocol Class Four (TP4).

**voiceband.** A transmission service with a bandwidth considered suitable for transmission of audio signals. The frequency range generally is 300 or 500 hertz to 3,000 or 3,400 hertz.

**voice digitization.** The conversion of analog voice signals into a digital form for transmission, processing, or storage.

**voice frequency.** The frequency range usually considered necessary for the effective transmission of human speech, typically 300 to 3,400 hertz.

**voice-grade channel**

**voice-grade channel.** A communications channel capable of properly transmitting the range of frequencies acceptable for voice communications, normally 300 to 3,400 hertz.

**voice-grade private line (VGPL).** A private analog line.

**VOTS.** *See* VMS OSI Transport Services.

**VPN.** *See* virtual private network.

**VQL.** *See* variable quantizing level.

**VRC.** *See* vertical redundancy check.

**VSAT.** *See* very small aperture terminal.

**V series recommendations.** A series of CCITT standards dealing mainly, but not exclusively, with modem interfaces. V series recommendations specify data rate, synchronous or asynchronous transmission, and control characteristics for each modem type.

**VTAM.** *See* Virtual Telecommunications Access Method.

**VT emulator.** Software or hardware that allows a device to imitate the characteristics of one of Digital Equipment Corp.'s VT family of video terminals.

**VTP.** *See* Virtual Terminal Protocol.

# W

**WACK.** *See* wait while acknowledge.

**wait while acknowledge (WACK).** A transmission control signal issued by a receiver to indicate that it has received a transmitted set of information such as a byte, frame, or block but that it has not had time to establish its accuracy. A WACK signal normally delays further transmission until another decision can be made.

**WAN.** *See* wide area network.

**Wangnet.** The network architecture used by Wang Laboratories Inc.

**watchdog timer.** A circuit used in Ethernet transceivers to ensure that transmission frames are never longer than the specified maximum length.

**WATS.** *See* wide area trunk services.

**waveform.** The shape of the wave formed when the instantaneous values of an alternating signal are plotted against time.

**wave-guide.** A type of conductor in the form of a tube used to transfer microwave radiation from one point to another in a contained manner.

**wavelength.** The distance between successive peaks of a sine wave. A sine wave is defined as an electromagnetic wave, whose amplitude is a sinusoidal function of time.

**wavelength-division multiplexing (WDM).** In fiber optics, a multiplexing technique that uses different optical frequencies for concurrent parallel data streams.

**WDM.** *See* wavelength-division multiplexing.

**WESTAR.** A family of communications satellites owned and operated by Western Union Corp.

**wet-T1.** A T1 circuit with a telephone company-powered interface.

**wide area network (WAN).** A network that extends over large distances and is normally supported by common carrier transmission services.

**wide area trunk services (WATS).** A telephone company service used to reduce the cost of long-distance calling.

**wideband.** A signal or channel whose frequency is higher than the frequency range normally considered to be voice grade. Frequencies from 4,000 hertz and up are considered to be in the wideband range.

**window.** The number of transmission entities such as blocks, messages, and packets that can be sent from transmitter to receiver without acknowledgment.

**wire center.** In token-ring technology, a point (for example, a box or closet) from which wiring radiates out to each attached device. The wiring center creates the ring.

**wire concentrator.** A conduit; a pipe within which a large number of individual wires are routed through a given space.

**wiring closet.** A room containing the individual network connections for all devices in a specific area.

**workgroup computing.** An approach to the supply of computer services whereby access to computer power and information is organized on a workgroup by workgroup basis. Such systems normally consist of computers of varying capabilities connected to a local area network.

**workstation.** A specially constructed device or a specially configured general-purpose computer which efficiently delivers a limited range of services to an end user. A workstation normally relies on other, more powerful computers to provide more general services.

**wrapping.** In token-ring networks, the process of bypassing cable faults without changing the logical order of the ring by using relays and additional wire circuits.

# X

**X3.** A series of ANSI data communications standards. X3 should not be confused with the CCITT X.3 specification for packet assembly/disassembly devices.

**X3.15.** The ANSI specification for the bit sequence of serial by bit ASCII transmission.

**X3.16.** The ANSI specification for the character structure and parity sense for serial by bit ASCII data transmission.

**X3.36.** The ANSI specification for synchronous high-speed data signaling.

**X3.79.** The ANSI specification for the determination of performance characteristics for transmission systems that use bit-oriented protocols.

**X3.92.** The ANSI specification for a data encryption algorithm.

**Xenix.** A version of UNIX developed for computers from Zenith Data Systems, a Groupe Bull Company.

**Xerox Network Services (XNS).** The upper-level service specifications for a network developed by Xerox Corp. to support its line of office automation products. XNS is popular with some personal computer network management software.

**Xerox Telecommunications Network (XTEN).** A digital electronic message service developed by Xerox Corp.

**XID frame.** A High-Level Data Link Control (HDLC) transmission frame used to transfer operational parameters between two or more stations.

**XMODEM.** An asynchronous data link control protocol in the public domain.

**XNS.** *See* Xerox Network Services.

**X-on/X-off.** An extension of the TTY protocol that uses additional Transmission On (X-on) and Transmission Off (X-off) characters to accommodate differences in speed between the transmitter and receiver.

**X/Open.** An organization dedicated to standardizing the upper layers of UNIX in order to create a common application environment and enhance system interoperability. *Address:* X/Open, San Francisco, CA 94111.

**XPC.** A set of protocols developed by British Telecom Tymnet to allow asynchronous terminals to connect to X.25 packet-switched network.

**XTEN.** *See* Xerox Telecommunications Network.

# Y-Z

**yellow alarm.** A transmission alarm condition on a T1 line.

**ZBTSI.** *See* zero-byte time-slot interchange.

**zero-bit insertion.** The insertion of additional zeros after a fixed number of ones in a transmission sequence to ensure that data will not be misinterpreted as controlling information. *See also* data transparency.

**zero-byte time-slot interchange (ZBTSI).** A control technique used in some T1 systems whereby information the about locations of all-zero bytes is contained in a defined area of the transmission frame.

**zero-code suppression.** Various techniques used to prevent the existence of eight consecutive zeros in a digital transmission frame. Zero-code suppression is essential for the proper operation of most T1 and higher-speed digital transmission systems.

# Numerics

**1Base-5.** A transmission medium specified by IEEE 802.3 that carries information at 1.0 Mbps in baseband form using twisted-pair conductors and accommodates 500-meter repeaterless runs.

**10Base-2.** A transmission medium specified by IEEE 802.3 that carries information at 10 Mbps in baseband form using low-cost coaxial cable and accommodates 200-meter repeaterless runs. Often called ThinWire Ethernet.

**10Base-5.** A transmission medium specified by IEEE 802.3 that carries information at 10 Mbps in baseband form using 50-ohm coaxial cable and accommodates 500-meter repeaterless runs. 10Base-5 was specified by the original Ethernet standards and is sometimes called ThickWire Ethernet.

**10Base-T.** A transmission medium specified by IEEE 802.3 that carries information at 10 Mbps in baseband form using twisted-pair conductors.